Jesus

BIBLIOGRAPHIES

Tremper Longman III
General Editor and Old Testament Editor

Craig A. Evans
New Testament Editor

1. Pentateuch
2. Historical Books
3. Poetry and Wisdom
4. Prophecy and Apocalyptic
5. Jesus
6. Synoptic Gospels
7. Johannine Writings
8. Acts
9. Pauline Writings
10. Hebrews and General Epistles
11. Old Testament Introduction
12. New Testament Introduction
13. Old Testament Theology
14. New Testament Theology

BIBLIOGRAPHIES No. 5

Jesus

Craig A. Evans

BAKER BOOK HOUSE

Grand Rapids, Michigan 49516

Address permission requests to:

Baker Book House
Box 6287
Grand Rapids, Michigan 49516-6287

Library of Congress Cataloging-in-Publication Data

Evans, Craig A.
    Jesus / Craig A. Evans.
        p.   cm. — (IBR bibliographies ; no. 5)
    Updated and abridged ed. of: Life of Jesus research. 1989.
    Includes bibliographical references and index.
    ISBN 0-8010-3218-0
    1. Jesus Christ—Biography—Bibliography. 2. Jesus Christ—Biogra-
phy—History and criticism. I. Evans, Craig A. Life of Jesus research.
II. Title. III. Series.
Z8455.E94   1992
[BT301.9]
016.2329'01—dc20   92-26565

Contents

Series Preface

With the proliferation of journals and publishing houses dedicated to biblical studies, it has become impossible for even the most dedicated scholar to keep in touch with the vast materials now available for research in all the different parts of the canon. How much more difficult for the minister, rabbi, student, or interested layperson! Herein lies the importance of bibliographies and in particular this series—IBR Bibliographies.

Bibliographies help guide students to works relevant to their research interests. They cut down the time needed to locate materials, thus providing the researcher with more time to read, assimilate, and write. These benefits are especially true for the IBR Bibliographies. First, the series is conveniently laid out along the major divisions of the canon, with four volumes planned on the Old Testament, six on the New Testament, and four on methodology (see page 2). Each volume will contain approximately five hundred entries, arranged under various topics to allow for ease of reference. Since the possible entries far exceed this number, the compiler of each volume must select the more important and helpful works for inclusion. Furthermore, the entries are briefly annotated in order to inform the reader about their contents more specifically, once again giving guidance to the appropriate material and saving time by preventing the all too typical "wild goose chase" in the library.

One of the problems with published bibliographies in the past is that they are soon out of date. The development of computer-based publishing has changed this, however, and it is the plan of the Institute for Biblical Research and Baker Book House to publish updates of each volume about every five years.

Since the series is designed primarily for American and British students, the emphasis is on works written in English, with a five-percent limit on titles not translated into English. Fortunately, a number of the most important foreign-language works have been translated into English, and wherever this is the case this information is included along with the original publication data. Again keeping in mind the needs of the student, we have decided to list the English translation before the original title (for chronological purposes, the titles are arranged according to the dates of their original publication).

These bibliographies are presented under the sponsorship of the Institute for Biblical Research (IBR), an organization of evangelical Christian scholars with specialties in both Old and New Testaments and their ancillary disciplines. The IBR has met annually since 1970; its name and constitution were adopted in 1973. Besides its annual meetings (normally held the evening and morning prior to the annual meeting of the Society of Biblical Literature), the institute publishes a journal, *Bulletin for Biblical Research*, and conducts regional study groups on various biblical themes in several areas of the United States and Canada. The Institute for Biblical Research encourages and fosters scholarly research among its members, all of whom are at a level to qualify for a university lectureship. Finally, the IBR and the series editor extend their thanks to Baker Book House for its efforts to bring this series to publication. In particular, we would like to thank David Aiken for his wise guidance in giving shape to the project.

Tremper Longman III
Westminster Theological Seminary

Author's Preface

The present bibliography has been prepared with the student not the scholar in mind. Its present form represents an updated and abridged version of my *Life of Jesus Research: An Annotated Bibliography* (New Testament Tools and Studies 13; Leiden: Brill, 1989), which contained some 1,300 items, many of them in a foreign language. This bibliography retains only the most important foreign items (approximately two-thirds of them have been omitted), but it adds several items that appeared between 1988 and 1991. Scholars and advanced students are encouraged to make use of the unabridged edition.

Jesus provides bibliography that concentrates on the most significant scholarship concerned with the problem of the historical Jesus and special topics. Every effort has been made to provide complete bibliographical information, that is, original language and edition, translations (in some cases) into other major languages, and most recent edition. Brief annotations are included with most of the bibliographic entries, which are listed in chronological order within each section (except §1.1). Annotations of multiple-author works vary in detail depending on the extent to which they are directly concerned with the historical Jesus. The introductions to chapters and sections are intended primarily for the beginning student, for it is assumed that the scholar and advanced student need no such introduction. Chapter 12 also includes excerpts from the most important extrabiblical sources that make reference to Jesus. An index to modern authors keyed to the numbered bibliographical items enables the reader to locate the works of a given scholar with ease.

A word of thanks is due Richard A. Wiebe, reference librarian of Trinity Western University, for conducting dozens of computer searches for bibliographical information. Without his assistance the writing of this volume would have been much more difficult and time-consuming. I would also like to thank my daughters Carrie and Jill for helping with the indexes.

Trinity Western University
Langley, British Columbia
March 1992

Abbreviations

CBQ	*Catholic Biblical Quarterly*
ExpTim	*Expository Times*
Interp	*Interpretation*
JETS	*Journal of the Evangelical Theological Society*
JR	*Journal of Religion*
JSNT	*Journal for the Study of the New Testament*
NovT	*Novum Testamentum*
NTS	*New Testament Studies*
SBLSP	*Society of Biblical Literature Seminar Papers*
SBT	Studies in Biblical Theology
SJT	*Scottish Journal of Theology*
SNTSMS	Society for New Testament Studies Monograph Series
WUNT	Wissenschaftliche Untersuchungen zum Neuen Testament
ZTK	*Zeitschrift für Theologie und Kirche*

1

Bibliographies and Surveys of Research

The items cited in chapter 1 are particularly valuable for their bibliographies and surveys of the scholarly problem of the historical Jesus, though many of the studies cited in the other chapters also provide helpful bibliographical material. Other reports of research will be will found in chapter 2. (Items in §1.1 are listed in alphabetical order, in contrast to the chronological order used throughout the rest of the book.)

1.1 Indexes

1   *Elenchus Bibliographicus Biblicus*. Rome: Pontifical Biblical Institute, 1968–present.

2   P.-E. Langevin (ed.). *Bibliographie Biblique*, vol. 1: *1930–1970*; vol. 2: *1930–1975*; vol. 3: *1930–1983*. Quebec: Les Presses de l'Université Laval, 1972, 1978, 1985.

3   B. M. Metzger. *Index to Periodical Literature on Christ and the Gospels*, pp. 40–51, 188–91. New Testament Tools and Studies 6. Leiden: Brill, 1966.

4   *New Testament Abstracts* 1 (1956)–present.

5   *Religion Index One* 13 (1977)–present.
     Formerly called *Index to Religious Periodical Literature* 1–12 (1949–76).

6   *Religion Index Two* 1 (1970)–present.

1.2 General Bibliography

7   A. Schweitzer. *The Quest of the Historical Jesus: A Critical Study of Its Progress from Reimarus to Wrede.* Translated by W. Montgomery. New York: Macmillan/London: Black, 1910. Reprinted 1954; New York: Macmillan, 1968 (introduction by J. M. Robinson); London: SCM, 1981. Original title: *Von Reimarus zu Wrede: Eine Geschichte des Leben-Jesu-Forschung.* Tübingen: Mohr, 1906. Second edition: *Die Geschichte der Leben-Jesu-Forschung.* Tübingen: Mohr, 1913. Sixth edition: 1951.

Outstanding survey of nineteenth-century quest. See comments below at #46.

8   C. C. McCown. *The Search for the Real Jesus: A Century of Historical Study.* New York: Scribner, 1940.

Discusses D. F. Strauss, Hegelianism, F. C. Baur, historiography, A. Harnack, and A. Schweitzer.

9   D. T. Rowlingson. "The Continuing Quest of the Historical Jesus." Pp. 42–69 in *New Testament Studies: Critical Essays in New Testament Study.* Edited by E. P. Booth. New York/Nashville: Abingdon-Cokesbury, 1942.

Reviews recent form- and source-critical work and several recent books on Jesus (1918–40).

10   H. Conzelmann. *Jesus.* Translated by J. R. Lord. Edited by J. Reumann. Philadelphia: Fortress, 1973. Original title: "Jesus Christus." Cols. 619–53 in *Religion in Geschichte und Gegenwart*, vol. 3. Edited by K. Galling et al. Third edition. Tübingen: Mohr, 1959.

11   H. K. McArthur. "Basic Issues: A Survey of Recent Gospel Research." *Interp* 18 (1964) 39–55.

12   H. C. Kee. "The Historical Jesus: A Survey of Literature (1959–65)." *Drew Gateway* 36 (1965–66) 44–49.

13   H. K. McArthur. *The Quest through the Centuries: The Search for the Historical Jesus.* Philadelphia: Fortress, 1966.

A survey of life-of-Jesus study.

14   H. Zahrnt. "The Rediscovery of the Historical Jesus." Pp. 253–94 in Zahrnt's *Question of God: Protestant Theology in the Twentieth Century.* Translated by R. A. Wilson. New

York: Harcourt, Brace & World, 1969. Original title: "Die Wiederentdeckung des historischen Jesus." Pp. 326–81 in Zahrnt's *Die Sache mit Gott: Die protestantische Theologie im 20. Jahrhundert.* Munich: Piper, 1966.

An excellent survey of the new quest.

15 N. Perrin. *Rediscovering the Teaching of Jesus.* New York: Harper & Row, 1967.

See pp. 249–66 for several brief, but very helpful, annotated bibliographies.

16 P. Grech. "Recent Developments in the Jesus of History Controversy." *Biblical Theology Bulletin* 1 (1971) 190–213.

17 G. Aulén. *Jesus in Contemporary Historical Research.* Translated by I. H. Hjelm. Philadelphia: Fortress/London: SPCK, 1976. Original title: *Jesus i nutida historisk forskning.* Second edition. Stockholm: Verbum, 1974.

Good critical survey and bibliography; observes an increasing tendency among scholars to view the Gospels as containing reliable historical material.

18 J. Reumann. "'Lives of Jesus' during the Great Quest for the Historical Jesus." *Indian Journal of Theology* 23 (1974) 33–59.

19 D. E. Aune. *Jesus and the Synoptic Gospels.* Theological Students Fellowship–Institute for Biblical Research Bibliographic Study Guides. Madison: Theological Students Fellowship, 1980.

Annotated bibliography is provided; see pp. 1–4 and 42–48.

20 D. L. Pals. *The Victorian "Lives" of Jesus.* Trinity University Monograph Series in Religion 7. San Antonio: Trinity University Press, 1982.

As a counterpart to Schweitzer's German focus (see #7), Pals surveys the British quest of the historical Jesus.

21 W. B. Tatum. *In Quest of Jesus: A Guidebook.* Atlanta: John Knox, 1982.

Provides a good introductory survey and basic bibliography; pays close attention to the crucial issues.

22 P. W. Hollenbach. "Recent Historical Jesus Studies and the Social Sciences." *SBLSP* 22 (1983) 61–78.

23   C. Brown. *Jesus in European Protestant Thought, 1778–1860.*
         Studies in Historical Theology 1. Durham, N.C.: Labyrinth,
         1985. Reprinted Grand Rapids: Baker, 1988.
         Critical survey and bibliography; assessment in many
         ways quite different from that of Schweitzer (see #7).

24   J. H. Charlesworth. "Research on the Historical Jesus." *Pro-
         ceedings of the Irish Biblical Association* 9 (1985) 19–37.
         Reviews and discusses work from 1980 to 1984.

25   D. J. Harrington. *The New Testament: A Bibliography,* pp.
         81–89. Theological and Biblical Resources 2. Wilmington,
         Del.: Glazier, 1985.

26   W. S. Kissinger. *The Lives of Jesus: A History and Bibliogra-
         phy.* New York: Garland, 1985.
         Helpful introductory survey of the scholarly quest; bibli-
         ography of lives of Jesus, however, is cluttered with hun-
         dreds of unscholarly contributions.

27   W. G. Kümmel. *Dreissig Jahre Jesusforschung (1950–80).*
         Bonner biblische Beiträge 60. Bonn: Hanstein, 1985.
         Collection of bibliographical articles originally published
         in *Theologische Rundschau* 31 (1966) 15–46, 289–315; 40
         (1975) 289–336; 41 (1976–77) 197–258, 295–363; 43 (1978)
         105–61, 233–65; 45 (1980) 40–84, 293–337; 46 (1981) 317–
         63; 47 (1982) 136–65, 348–83; 53 (1988) 229–49; 54 (1989)
         1–53; 55 (1990) 21–45; 56 (1991) 27–53. One of the most
         valuable resources for research on the historical Jesus.

28   J. H. Charlesworth. "From Barren Mazes to Gentle Rappings:
         The Emergence of Jesus Research." *Princeton Seminary Bul-
         letin* 7 (1986) 221–30.
         Survey with annotated bibliography; see his *Jesus within
         Judaism* (#33).

29   E. G. Lawler. *David Friedrich Strauss and His Critics: The
         Life of Jesus Debate in Early Nineteenth-Century German
         Journals.* New York: Lang, 1986.
         An invaluable aid to research on the nineteenth-century
         quest.

30   J. R. Michaels. "Off on a New Quest for the Historical Jesus."
         Books and Religion 14 (1986) 3–4.

Surveys recent work.

31 C. A. Evans. "Jesus of Nazareth: Who Do Scholars Say That He Is?" *Crux* 23/4 (1987) 15–19.

Review article of recent contributions by G. Vermes, B. F. Meyer, A. E. Harvey, E. P. Sanders, and others.

32 C. A. Evans. "The Historical Jesus and Christian Faith: A Critical Assessment of a Scholarly Problem." *Christian Scholars Review* 18 (1988) 48–63.

Survey and bibliography.

33 J. H. Charlesworth. *Jesus within Judaism*. Anchor Bible Reference Library. Garden City, N.Y.: Doubleday, 1988.

Provides annotated bibliography of recent scholarship. See comments below at #138.

34 C. A. Evans. *Life of Jesus Research: An Annotated Bibliography*. New Testament Tools and Studies 13. Leiden: Brill, 1989.

Provides annotated bibliography of 1,300 scholarly items. In contrast to the present work, contains numerous foreign-language entries.

2

Classic Studies

The beginning of life-of-Jesus research is traced back to the posthumous publication of seven writings of H. S. Reimarus, particularly fragment 7 entitled *Von dem Zwecke Jesu und seiner Jünger* (On the aim of Jesus and his disciples), published in 1778 (see #35). Reimarus believed that Jesus had not anticipated his death, but had hoped to become Israel's earthly Messiah. After the crucifixion, his disciples reformulated Jesus' teachings and proclaimed his resurrection and return. This critical assessment of the gospel story of Jesus inaugurated the scholarly quest of the historical Jesus.

The nineteenth-century "old quest" of the historical Jesus represents the first major phase of this scholarly quest. In his *Das Leben Jesu kritisch bearbeitet* (The Life of Jesus critically examined; 1835–36; see #38), D. F. Strauss argued that the Gospels do not present history, whether embellished with supernatural elements (so the liberals) or not (so the conservatives), but present myth. Liberal and conservative scholars alike opposed this radical skepticism and searched for what was then regarded as "historical" material. For a short time the Gospel of John was viewed as the best source, since it lacked some of the miraculous features of the Synoptics (e.g., virgin birth, demon exorcisms), which many scholars viewed as mythological. But F. C. Baur's *Kritische Untersuchungen über die kanonischen Evangelien* (Critical investigations of the canonical Gospels) (Tübingen:

18

Fues, 1847), which concluded that John was written late in the second century, brought an end to this thinking. It was then concluded that the historical Jesus would have to be found in the Synoptic Gospels after all. In his *Die synoptischen Evangelien: Ihr Ursprung und geschichtlicher Charakter* (The Synoptic Gospels: Their origin and historical character; 1863; see #40), H. J. Holtzmann showed that Mark was written first and that Matthew and Luke used it (or *Urmarkus*) and another source of sayings (eventually called "Q," for the German word *Quelle* ["source"]). Mark and Q became the sources from which a historical Jesus might be reconstructed. Most scholars assumed that these sources were relatively free from mythological embellishment.

With the appearance of certain publications at the turn of the century, it became evident that the old quest had not been successful. M. Kähler's *Der sogenannte historische Jesus und der geschichtliche, biblische Christus* (The so-called historical Jesus and the historic, biblical Christ; 1892; see #44) argued that the historical Jesus of the nineteenth-century quest bore little resemblance to, or had little significance for, the Christ of faith. That same year J. Weiss published *Die Predigt Jesu vom Reiche Gottes* (The preaching of Jesus concerning the kingdom of God; see #45), in which he argued that Jesus was not a social reformer, but an apocalyptic prophet who summoned people to repent because judgment was near. In 1901 W. Wrede published *Das Messiasgeheimnis in den Evangelien* (The messianic secret in the Gospels) (Göttingen: Vandenhoeck & Ruprecht, 1901), in which he argued that, far from being a simple historical account, Mark's Gospel was a theologically oriented document comparable to John's Gospel. Finally, the appearance of A. Schweitzer's *Von Reimarus zu Wrede* (From Reimarus to Wrede; 1906; see #7), in which he concluded that Jesus had died a deluded apocalyptic fanatic, led many scholars and theologians to believe that the quest of the historical Jesus was impossible (so the form critics) and perhaps even illegitimate (so many neoorthodox theologians). Speaking as a form critic, in 1926 R. Bultmann stated that "we can now know almost nothing concerning the life and personality of Jesus" (#49, p. 8). The popular neoorthodox theologian E. Brunner claimed that "the Christian faith does not arise out of

the picture of the historical Jesus" and that "the Jesus of history
is not the same as the Christ of faith" (*The Mediator* [London:
Lutterworth, 1934; repr. Philadelphia: Westminster, 1957], p.
159). Moreover, the recognition, thanks largely to Schweitzer,
that the lives of Jesus of the old quest reflected the issues and
emphases of each generation of scholars (the major error of the
old quest) led many to suppose that the objectivity necessary for
a truly fair portrait of Jesus simply could not be had. Therefore,
in many circles the scholarly quest was abandoned.

When in 1953 E. Käsemann read his paper "Das Problem des
historischen Jesus" (The problem of the historical Jesus; see #54),
a new quest of the historical Jesus was inaugurated among Bult-
mannian scholars. Käsemann argued that a new quest, one that
was careful to avoid the errors of the old quest, was historically
possible and theologically necessary. A link between the Christ
of faith and the Jesus of history was necessary if Christianity
were to avoid lapsing into a form of Docetic Gnosticism. While
Käsemann emphasized the recovery of certain authentic sayings
of Jesus, E. Fuchs (see #56) argued for the presence of certain
authentic actions or attitudes. Other Bultmannians to participate in the new quest included H. Conzelmann (#58), E. Dinkler
(#78), H. Braun (#85), G. Ebeling (#61), and J. M. Robinson (#59).
The new quest is part of what is sometimes referred to as the
"post-Bultmannian" movement.

Not all scholars, however, felt constrained by the strictures of
Bultmann and his pupils. British scholars such as T. W. Manson
(#53) and C. H. Dodd (#60) continued to pursue the historical
Jesus with few of the theological and philosophical concerns that
characterized their German counterparts. They tended to be far
less skeptical of the historical value of the Gospels and far less
inclined to sacrifice sound principles of historiography for the
philosophical fads of the time.

This chapter, beginning with Reimarus and ending with Dodd,
presents the "classic" studies in life-of-Jesus research. Life-of-
Jesus research has taken giant strides since the appearance of
Dodd's work in 1970, but which books from this period will
come to be viewed as classics is difficult to forecast. The introduction to chapter 3 lists works that are judged to represent the
most important, and potentially most lasting, works in English.

35 H. S. Reimarus. *Fragments from Reimarus, Consisting of Brief Critical Remarks on the Object of Jesus and His Disciples as Seen in the New Testament.* Translated by G. E. Lessing. Edited by C. Voysey. London: Williams & Norgate, 1879. New edition: *Reimarus: Fragments.* Translated by R. S. Fraser. Edited by C. H. Talbert. Lives of Jesus Series. Philadelphia: Fortress, 1970. Original title: *Von dem Zwecke Jesu und seiner Jünger: Noch ein Fragment des Wolfenbüttelschen Ungenannten; Fragment 7.* Edited by G. E. Lessing. Braunschweig: [No publisher listed], 1778.

The first critical attempt to distinguish a historical Jesus from the Jesus presented in the Gospels and assumed to lie behind Christology; part of a larger unpublished manuscript entitled "Apologie oder Schutzschrift für die vernünftigen Verehre Gottes."

36 J. G. Herder. *Vom Erlöser der Menschen: Nach unsern drei ersten Evangelien.* Riga: Hartknoch, 1796.

Offers a symbolic interpretation of the miracles in the Synoptic Gospels.

37 H. E. G. Paulus. *Das Leben Jesu, als Grundlage einer reinen Geschichte des Urchristentums.* 2 vols. Heidelberg: Winter, 1828.

Believes that a historical, nonsupernatural Jesus can be recovered from the Gospels.

38 D. F. Strauss. *The Life of Jesus Critically Examined.* 3 vols. Translated by G. Eliot. London: Chapman, 1846. Reprinted: Edited by P. C. Hodgson. Lives of Jesus Series. Philadelphia: Fortress, 1972/London: SCM, 1973. Original title: *Das Leben Jesu kritisch bearbeitet.* 2 vols. Tübingen: Osiander, 1835–36. Third edition: 1838–39. Reprinted 1984.

Responding to the rationalist approaches of J. G. Herder (#36) and H. E. G. Paulus (#37), the gospel portrait of Jesus is viewed as mythological, with little of the Jesus of history recoverable.

39 J. E. Kuhn. *Das Leben Jesu wissenschaftlich bearbeitet.* Mainz: Kupferberg, 1838.

An early Roman Catholic response to Strauss (#38); argues that the Gospels are historical, but not in the ordinary sense of history, for the Gospels give us "sacred history."

40 H. J. Holtzmann. *Die synoptischen Evangelien: Ihr Ursprung und geschichtlicher Charakter.* Leipzig: Engelmann, 1863.

Although chiefly concerned with the origin and relationship of the Synoptic Gospels, there is a chapter on the historical Jesus entitled "Lebensbild Jesu nach der Quelle A [i.e., *Urmarkus*]" (pp. 468–96). In this chapter Holtzmann responds to Strauss and the scholarship from the 1830s to the 1860s. Holtzmann also offers his own sketch of the historical Jesus based upon Mark's Gospel.

41 E. Rénan. *The Life of Jesus.* Translated by C. E. Wilbour. London: Trübner, 1864. Reprinted New York: Random, 1955. Original title: *La Vie de Jésus.* Paris: Michel Lévy Frères, 1863.

The first major French work on the quest. Unlike most German studies, this work is romantic.

42 D. F. Strauss. *A New Life of Jesus.* London/Edinburgh: Williams & Norgate, 1865. Original title: *Das Leben Jesu für das deutsche Volk.* Leipzig: Brockhaus, 1864. Third edition: 1874.

Less radical than his earlier work, more in line with the contemporary liberal viewpoint. See the third edition of *Das Leben Jesu kritisch bearbeitet* (#38).

43 D. F. Strauss. *The Christ of Faith and the Jesus of History: A Critique of Schleiermacher's "Life of Jesus."* Translated by L. E. Keck. Lives of Jesus Series. Philadelphia: Fortress, 1977. Original title: *Der Christus des Glaubens und der Jesus der Geschichte: Eine Kritik des schleiermacher'schen Lebens Jesu.* Berlin: Duncker, 1865.

Strauss faults Schleiermacher for failing to approach the subject free from presuppositions and for thinking that a fully human Jesus could nevertheless "stand above the whole of humanity."

44 M. Kähler. *The So-called Historical Jesus and the Historic, Biblical Christ.* Translated and edited by C. E. Braaten. Philadelphia: Fortress, 1964. Reprinted 1988. Original title: *Der* *sogenannte historische Jesus und der geschichtliche, biblische Christus.* Leipzig: Deichert, 1892. Second edition: 1896. Calls into question the relevance of the so-called historical Jesus for Christian faith, noting the wide gap between the critical reconstruction of the historical Jesus of the nineteenth-century quest and the theological confession of the church. Concludes that the Gospels simply do not offer the information necessary for the biography that so many have attempted to write.

45 J. Weiss. *Jesus' Proclamation of the Kingdom of God.* Translated by R. H. Hiers and D. L. Holland. Lives of Jesus Series. Philadelphia: Fortress, 1971. Reprinted Chico, Calif.: Scholars Press, 1985. Original title: *Die Predigt Jesu vom Reiche Gottes.* Göttingen: Vandenhoeck & Ruprecht, 1892. Second edition: 1900. Third edition edited by F. Hahn; introduction by R. Bultmann: 1964.

Argues that Jesus' preaching was apocalyptic, not social.

46 A. Schweitzer. *The Quest of the Historical Jesus: A Critical Study of Its Progress from Reimarus to Wrede.* Translated by W. Montgomery. New York: Macmillan/London: Black, 1910. Reprinted 1954; New York: Macmillan, 1968 (with introduction by J. M. Robinson); London: SCM, 1981. Original title: *Von Reimarus zu Wrede: Eine Geschichte des Leben-Jesu-Forschung.* Tübingen: Mohr, 1906. Second edition: *Die Geschichte der Leben-Jesu-Forschung.* Tübingen: Mohr, 1913. Sixth edition: 1951.

Masterful survey of nineteenth-century quest; proposes that Jesus be understood in terms of "thoroughgoing" eschatology. Concludes that Jesus expected the kingdom to appear during his ministry; but when it did not, he died as a disillusioned fanatic (see pp. 370–71 of the English translation).

47 J. Klausner. *Jesus of Nazareth: His Life, Times, and Teaching.* Translated by H. Danby. New York/London: Macmillan, 1925. Third edition: 1952. Original title: *Yeshu ha-Notzri.* 2 vols. Jerusalem: Stybel, 1922 [Hebrew].

One of the first serious attempts to understand Jesus against a Jewish background; concludes that "Jesus was convinced of his messiahship: of this there is no doubt; were it not so he would have been nothing more than a mere deceiver and imposter—and such men do not make history" (p. 342).

48 M. Goguel. *The Life of Jesus*. Translated by O. Wyon. London: Unwin, 1926. Reprinted New York: Macmillan, 1933. Reprinted as *Jesus and the Origins of Christianity*. 2 vols. New York: Harper Torchbooks, 1960 (introduction by C. L. Mitton). Original title: *La Vie de Jésus*. Paris: Payot, 1925.

Argues that Jesus broke with John the Baptist over the question of repentance and grace, that Jesus' preaching of the kingdom was not apocalyptic, and that Jesus ministered in Jerusalem about six months (instead of one week.

49 R. Bultmann. *Jesus and the Word*. Translated by L. P. Smith and E. H. Lantero. New York: Scribner, 1934/London: Nicholson & Watson, 1935. Reprinted London: Collins, 1958. Original title: *Jesus*. Berlin: Deutsche Bibliothek, 1926.

Bultmann's classic statement of Jesus' relationship to the Christian message; very skeptical of the historical content of the Gospels: "I think that we can now know almost nothing concerning the life and personality of Jesus" (p. 8).

50 H. J. Cadbury. *The Peril of Modernizing Jesus*. New York: Macmillan, 1937. Reprinted London: SPCK, 1962.

Warns against reading modern ideas into the historical Jesus. To avoid this error it is necessary to (1) recognize our own prejudices, (2) learn the mentality of Jesus' times, and (3) study the Gospels critically.

51 M. Dibelius. *Jesus*. Translated by C. B. Hedrick and F. C. Grant. Philadelphia: Westminster, 1949. Reprinted London: SCM, 1963. Original title: *Jesus*. Berlin: de Gruyter, 1939. Second edition: 1949.

Jesus' ministry is a sign of the presence of the kingdom of God; the crucifixion is evidence that Jesus understood himself as the Messiah.

52 N. A. Dahl. "The Problem of the Historical Jesus." Translated by C. E. Braaten and R. A. Harrisville. Pp. 138–71 in *Kerygma and History: A Symposium on the Theology of Rudolf Bultmann*. Edited by C. E. Braaten and R. A. Harrisville.

Nashville: Abingdon, 1962. Reprinted in Dahl's *Crucified Messiah and Other Essays*, pp. 48–89, 173–74. Minneapolis: Augsburg, 1974. Original title: "Problemet den historiske Jesus." Pp. 156–202 in Dahl's *Rett laere og kjetterske meninger*. Oslo: Land og Kirke, 1953. Expanded German version: "Der historische Jesus als geschichtswissenschaftliches und theologisches Problem." *Kerygma und Dogma* 1 (1955) 104–32.

Finds link between historical Jesus and Christ of faith, for the former anticipated his death and attempted to interpret its significance.

53 T. W. Manson. *The Servant-Messiah: A Study of the Public Ministry of Jesus*. Cambridge: Cambridge University Press, 1953.

Argues that the crisis that Jesus faced was avoiding being recognized as a militaristic Messiah; the kingdom was realized in his ministry of love and service.

54 E. Käsemann. "The Problem of the Historical Jesus." Pp. 15–47 in Käsemann's *Essays on New Testament Themes*. Translated by W. J. Montague. SBT 41. Naperville, Ill.: Allenson/London: SCM, 1964. Original title: "Das Problem des historischen Jesus." *ZTK* 51 (1954) 125–53. Reprinted in Käsemann's *Exegetische Versuche und Besinnungen*, vol. 1, pp. 187–214. Göttingen: Vandenhoeck & Ruprecht, 1960.

The classic paper read in 1953 at the gathering of "old Marburgers" and is credited with launching the new quest; expresses dissatisfaction with R. Bultmann's position and offers a "corrective."

55 G. Bornkamm. *Jesus of Nazareth*. Translated by I. McLuskey, F. McLuskey, and J. M. Robinson. New York: Harper & Row/London: Hodder & Stoughton, 1960. Reprinted 1973. Original title: *Jesus von Nazareth*. Urban-Bücher 19. Stuttgart: Kohlhammer, 1956. Eleventh edition: 1977.

Classic statement from the "post-Bultmannian" perspective. See the review article by L. E. Keck in *JR* 49 (1969) 1–17. Also translated into Japanese (1961), Danish (1963), Dutch (1963), Italian (1968), French (1973), Spanish (1975), and Portuguese (1976). Chapters 1 ("Faith and History in the Gospels") and 3 ("Jesus of Nazareth") reprinted in *In Search of the Historical Jesus* (ed. H. K. McArthur; New York: Scribner, 1969/London: SPCK, 1970), pp. 41–53 and 164–73. Original of chapter 1 ("Glaube und Geschichte in den Evangelien") reprinted in *Glauben heute* (ed. G. Otto; Stundenbücher Sonderband 48; Hamburg: Furche, 1965), pp. 96–112.

56   E. Fuchs. "The Quest of the Historical Jesus." Pp. 11–31 in Fuchs's *Studies of the Historical Jesus*. Translated by A. Scobie. SBT 42. Naperville, Ill.: Allenson/London: SCM, 1964. Original title: "Die Frage nach dem historischen Jesus." *ZTK* 53 (1956) 210–29. Reprinted in Fuchs's *Zur Frage nach dem historischen Jesus*, pp. 143–67. Gesammelte Aufsätze 2. Tübingen: Mohr, 1960.

Christology is to be found in Jesus' attitude and conduct toward sinners; faith in Jesus is to repeat Jesus' decision to have faith.

57   J. Jeremias. "The Present Position in the Controversy concerning the Problem of the Historical Jesus." *ExpTim* 69 (1957–58) 333–39. Revised and reprinted in Jeremias's *Problem of the Historical Jesus*. Facet Books, Biblical Series 13. Philadelphia: Fortress, 1964. Second edition: 1969. Original title: "Der gegenwärtige Stand der Debatte um das Problem des historischen Jesus." *Wissenschaftliche Zeitschrift der Ernst Moritz Arndt–Universität Greifswald* 6 (1956–57) 165–70. Revised and reprinted in *Der historische Jesus und der kerygmatische Christus: Beiträge zum Christusverständnis in Forschung und Verkündigung* [#68], pp. 12–25. Edited by H. Ristow and K. Matthiae. Berlin: Evangelische Verlaganstalt, 1960. Expanded as Jeremias's *Das Problem des historischen Jesus*. Edited by T. Schlatter. Calwer Hefte 32. Stuttgart: Calwer, 1960. Sixth edition: 1969.

Concise presentation of the problems and proposals of the new quest; argues that the quest of the historical Jesus is the most important task of New Testament scholarship.

58   H. Conzelmann. *Jesus*. Translated by J. R. Lord. Edited by J. Reumann. Philadelphia: Fortress, 1973. Original title: "Jesus Christus." Cols. 619–53 in *Religion in Geschichte und Gegen-*

wart, vol. 3. Edited by K. Galling et al. Third edition. Tübingen: Mohr, 1959.

Classic assessment of historical-Jesus scholarship; good bibliography.

59 J. M. Robinson. *A New Quest of the Historical Jesus*. SBT 25. Naperville, Ill.: Allenson/London: SCM, 1959. Reprinted Missoula, Mont.: Scholars Press, 1979. Reprinted as *A New Quest of the Historical Jesus and Other Essays*. Philadelphia: Fortress, 1983. German edition: *Kerygma und historischer Jesus*. Translated by H.-D. Knigge. Zurich/Stuttgart: Zwingli, 1960. Second edition: 1967.

An assessment of the post-Bultmannian new quest of the historical Jesus. Robinson argues that the new quest is both historically possible and theologically legitimate.

60 C. H. Dodd. *The Founder of Christianity*. New York/London: Macmillan, 1970.

Takes into account the first-century Palestinian context well; emphasizes Jesus' personal characteristics and his desire to establish a community worthy of being called "the people of God."

3

General Discussion

In the 1960s and 1970s life-of-Jesus research was continued, but often the emphasis was placed on Jesus as a social or political figure, rather than as a figure relevant for faith (as the emphasis had been during the new quest). For example, Jesus became the champion of the poor and the oppressed and as such is sometimes the inspiration for liberation theologies. Although the legitimacy of some of this work cannot be denied, one cannot help but wonder if the basic error of the old quest is recurring. Some of the studies that appeared in the 1970s and 1980s, however, seem to represent a return to a quest not governed by theological or political agendas.

The emphasis now is on seeing Jesus against the background of first-century Palestinian Judaism. Among these are works by C. H. Dodd (#60), J. Bowker (#94), G. Vermes (#95, #127), A. E. Harvey (#115), G. S. Sloyan (#120), M. J. Borg (#123), E. P. Sanders (#132), R. A. Horsley (#136), J. H. Charlesworth (#138), B. Witherington III (#363), M. de Jonge (#151), and J. P. Meier (#152). Unlike the new quest, which had emphasized discontinuity between Jesus and his contemporaries, the more recent studies tend to emphasize continuity. It would appear that these studies reflected and in some cases apparently ushered in a new phase in life-of-Jesus research.

61   G. Ebeling. "The Question of the Historical Jesus and the Problem of Christology." Pp. 288–304 in Ebeling's *Word and*

Faith. Translated by J. W. Leitch. Philadelphia: Fortress, 1963. Original title: "Die Frage nach dem historischen Jesus und das Problem der Christologie." *ZTK* 56 (1959) 14–30. Reprinted in Ebeling's *Wort und Glaube,* pp. 300–318. Tübingen: Mohr, 1960.

> Emphasizes continuity between Jesus of history and Christ of faith.

62 A. Wikgren. "Biography and Christology in the Gospels." *Studia Evangelica* 1 [= Texte und Untersuchungen 73] (1959) 115–25.

> Argues that the Gospels evince an interest in biographical detail that does not likely derive from Christology only, but from the historical Jesus.

63 W. D. Davies. "A Quest to Be Resumed in New Testament Studies." *Union Seminary Quarterly Review* 15 (1959–60) 83–98.

> Because the Gospels proclaim the Jesus of history, even though obviously reflecting the early church's kerygma, the quest for the historical Jesus is an essential component of Christian theology. Concludes that the quest is therefore imperative.

64 O. Cullmann. "Out of Season Remarks on the 'Historical Jesus' of the Bultmann School." Translated by J. L. Martyn. *Union Seminary Quarterly Review* 16 (1960–61) 131–48. Original title: "Unzeitgemässe Bemerkungen zum 'historischen Jesus' der Bultmann-Schule." Pp. 266–80 in *Der historische Jesus und der kerygmatische Christus: Beiträge zum Christusverständnis in Forschung und Verkündigung* [#68]. Edited by H. Ristow and K. Matthiae. Berlin: Evangelische Verlaganstalt, 1960.

> Argues that the existentialist approach to hermeneutics of R. Bultmann and pupils hinders the efforts of the new quest, a quest which is otherwise appropriate and necessary.

65 W. R. Farmer and N. Perrin. "The Kerygmatic Theology and the Question of the Historical Jesus." *Religion in Life* 29 (1960) 86–97.

A discussion of the contributions of R. Bultmann (#49), E. Käsemann (#54), G. Bornkamm (#55), and E. Fuchs (#56), plus Bultmann's response to his pupils (#77, pp. 15–42).

66   E. Fuchs. *Zur Frage nach dem historischen Jesus*. Gesammelte Aufsätze 2. Tübingen: Mohr, 1960. Selections translated in Fuchs's *Studies of the Historical Jesus*. Translated by A. Scobie. SBT 42. Naperville, Ill.: Allenson/London: SCM, 1964.

Collection of several articles, some of which are cited elsewhere (see #56).

67   W. Marxsen. *The Beginnings of Christology: A Study in Its Problems*. Translated by P. J. Achtemeier. Facet Books, Biblical Series 22. Philadelphia: Fortress, 1969. Second edition: 1979. Original title: *Anfangsprobleme der Christologie*. Gütersloh: Mohn, 1960.

Searches for the link between the Jesus of history and the church's Christology; concludes that the message of the historical Jesus is a constituent part of the post-Easter kerygma.

68   H. Ristow and K. Matthiae (eds.). *Der historische Jesus und der kerygmatische Christus: Beiträge zum Christusverständnis in Forschung und Verkündigung*. Berlin: Evangelische Verlaganstalt, 1960.

Very important collection of studies, including J. Jeremias, "Der gegenwärtigen Stand der Debatte um das Problem des historischen Jesus" (pp. 12–25; see #57); R. Marlé, "Der Christus des Glaubens und der historische Jesus" (pp. 26–38); W. G. Kümmel, "Das Problem des geschichtlichen Jesus in der gegenwärtigen Forschungslage" (pp. 39–53); E. Heitsch, "Jesus aus Nazareth als Christus" (pp. 62–86); H. Conzelmann, "Jesus von Nazareth und der Glaube an den Auferstandenen" (pp. 188–99); B. Reicke, "Der Fleischgewordene: Zur Diskussion über den 'historischen' Jesus und den kerygmatischen Christus" (pp. 208–18); H. Diem, "Der irdische Jesus und der Christus des Glaubens" (pp. 219–32); R. Bultmann, "Das Verhältnis des urchristlichen Christuskerygmas zum historischen Jesus" (pp. 233–35; see #77, pp. 15–42); O. Cullmann, "Unzeitgemässe

Bemerkungen zum 'historischen Jesus' der Bultmann-Schule" (pp. 266–80); G. Bornkamm, "Glaube und Geschichte in den Evangelien" (pp. 281–88); and E. Fuchs, "Die Verkündigung Jesu: Der Spruch von den Raben" (pp. 385–88).

69 H. Zahrnt. *The Historical Jesus.* Translated by J. S. Bowden. New York: Harper & Row/London: Collins, 1963. Original title: *Es begann mit Jesus von Nazareth: Die Frage nach dem historischen Jesus.* Gütersloh: Mohn, 1960.

Very helpful survey of the life-of-Jesus research, especially with regard to the new quest.

70 R. M. Grant. *The Earliest Lives of Jesus.* New York: Harper & Row/London: SPCK, 1961.

Assessment of interest in historical Jesus among early church fathers.

71 F. Hahn, W. Lohff, and G. Bornkamm. *What Can We Know about Jesus? Essays on the New Quest.* Translated by G. Foley. Philadelphia: Fortress, 1969. Original title: *Die Frage nach dem historischen Jesus.* Evangelisches Forum 2. Göttingen: Vandenhoeck & Ruprecht, 1962.

Three contributions by Hahn, "The Quest of the Historical Jesus and the Special Character of the Sources Available to Us" (pp. 9–48; original title: "Die Frage nach dem historischen Jesus und die Eigenart der uns zur Verfügung stehenden Quellen" [pp. 7–40]); Lohff, "The Significance for Faith of the Philosophical Quest for Jesus" (pp. 49–68; original title: "Die Bedeutung der philosophische Frage nach Jesus für den Glauben" [pp. 41–56]); and Bornkamm, "The Significance of the Historical Jesus for Faith" (pp. 69–86; original title: "Die Bedeutung des historischen Jesus für den Glauben" [pp. 57–71]).

72 J. Jervell. *The Continuing Search for the Historical Jesus.* Translated by H. E. Kaasa. Minneapolis: Augsburg, 1965. Original title: *Den historiske Jesus.* Oslo: Land og Kirke, 1962. New edition: *Historiens Jesus.* Oslo: Land og Kirke, 1978.

Concludes that Jesus "claimed to represent God in an exclusive and decisive way" (p. 78).

73   T. W. Manson. "The Life of Jesus: A Study of the Available Materials." Pp. 13–27 in Manson's *Studies in the Gospels and Epistles*. Edited by M. Black. Philadelphia: Westminster/ Manchester: Manchester University Press, 1962.

Assesses the nature of the materials from which one can recover the historical Jesus; sees the Gospel of Mark as providing the framework of Jesus' teaching and Q the details of his teaching. Since Mark and Q are independent and complement one another, we may conclude that they are historically reliable.

74   W. G. Kümmel. "Jesus und Paulus." *NTS* 10 (1963–64) 163–81.

Criticizes the views of W. Schmithals and others; argues that there is more continuity between Jesus and Paul.

75   G. Bornkamm. "The Problem of the Historical Jesus and the Kerygmatic Christ." *Studia Evangelica* 3 [= Texte und Untersuchungen 88] (1964) 33–44.

A succinct statement of the points of disagreement between G. Bornkamm and R. Bultmann.

76   G. Bornkamm. "The Risen Lord and the Earthly Jesus: Matthew 28.16–20." Pp. 203–29 in *The Future of Our Religious Past: Essays in Honour of Rudolf Bultmann*. Edited by J. M. Robinson. Translated by C. E. Carlston and R. P. Scharlemann. New York: Harper & Row, 1971. Original title: "Der Auferstandene und der Irdische: Mt 28,16–20." Pp. 171–91 in *Zeit und Geschichte: Dankesgabe an Rudolf Bultmann zum 80. Geburtstag*. Edited by E. Dinkler. Tübingen: Mohr, 1964.

Argues that the "authority" claim of the risen Christ, coming where it does in a pericope devoid of characteristic apocalyptic and christological details, provides a strong link with the historical Jesus who acted with authority.

77   C. E. Braaten and R. A. Harrisville (eds.). *The Historical Jesus and the Kerygmatic Christ: Essays on the New Quest of the Historical Jesus*. Nashville: Abingdon, 1964.

Contains several significant studies, including R. Bultmann, "The Primitive Christian Kerygma and the Historical Jesus" (pp. 15–42); E. Stauffer, "The Relevance of the Historical Jesus" (pp. 43–53); H. Conzelmann, "The

Method of the Life-of-Jesus Research" (pp. 54–68); H. Braun, "The Significance of Qumran for the Problem of the Historical Jesus" (pp. 69–78); C. E. Braaten, "Martin Kähler on the Historic Biblical Christ" (pp. 79–105); H.-W. Bartsch, "The Historical Problem of the Life of Jesus" (pp. 106–141); H. Ott, "The Historical Jesus and the Ontology of History" (pp. 142–71); and V. A. Harvey and S. M. Ogden, "How New Is the 'New Quest of the Historical Jesus'?" (pp. 197–242). Many of these studies appeared earlier in German: Braun's and Stauffer's in *Der historische Jesus und der kerygmatische Christus: Beiträge zum Christusverständnis in Forschung und Verkündigung* (ed. H. Ristow and K. Matthiae; Berlin: Evangelische Verlaganstalt, 1960); Bultmann's as *Das Verhältnis der urchristlichen Christusbotschaft zum historischen Jesus* (Heidelberg: Winter, 1960; 3d ed., 1962).

78 E. Dinkler. "Peter's Confession and the 'Satan' Saying: The Problem of Jesus' Messiahship." Pp. 169–202 in *The Future of Our Religious Past: Essays in Honour of Rudolf Bultmann*. Edited by J. M. Robinson. Translated by C. E. Carlston and R. P. Scharlemann. New York: Harper & Row, 1971. Original title: "Petrusbekenntnis und Satanswort: Das Problem der Messianität Jesu." Pp. 127–53 in *Zeit und Geschichte: Dankesgabe an Rudolf Bultmann zum 80. Geburtstag*. Edited by E. Dinkler. Tübingen: Mohr, 1964.

Argues that when Marcan and Christian elements are removed, we discover that Jesus rebuked Peter for identifying him as the Messiah of popular Jewish expectation (Mark 8:29, 33).

79 R. P. Martin. "The New Quest of the Historical Jesus." Pp. 25–45 in *Jesus of Nazareth: Saviour and Lord*. Edited by C. F. H. Henry. Grand Rapids: Eerdmans, 1966.

Summarizes and evaluates the new quest.

80 C. K. Barrett. *Jesus and the Gospel Tradition*. Philadelphia: Fortress, 1968/London: SPCK, 1967.

Fairly optimistic assessment of the general reliability of the Gospels; concludes that Jesus anticipated suffering and dying in behalf of his disciples and the righteous of

Israel, but hoped and prayed for God's intervention, either immediately before death or soon after.

81   S. G. F. Brandon. *Jesus and the Zealots: A Study of the Political Factor in Primitive Christianity.* New York: Scribner/ Manchester: Manchester University Press, 1967.

Argues that although Jesus was not himself a zealot, the presence of Simon the Zealot among the Twelve indicates that zealot principles were not incompatible with Jesus' views, and this is probably why Jesus was executed by the Romans for sedition. See J. G. Griffiths in *NTS* 19 (1972–73) 483–85.

82   M. Hengel. *The Charismatic Leader and His Followers.* Translated by J. Greig. New York: Crossroad/Edinburgh: T. & T. Clark, 1981. Original title: *Nachfolge und Charisma: Eine exegetisch-religionsgeschichtliche Studie zu Mt 8:21f. und Jesu Ruf in die Nachfolge.* Beihefte zur Zeitschrift für die neutestamentliche Wissenschaft 34. Berlin: Töpelmann, 1968.

Jesus' summons to discipleship is viewed as unique evidence that Jesus understood himself as Israel's Messiah.

83   F. T. Trotter (ed.). *Jesus and the Historian: Written in Honor of Ernest Cadman Colwell.* Philadelphia: Westminster, 1968.

The most significant articles include W. H. Brownlee, "Jesus and Qumran" (pp. 52–81); E. L. Titus, "The Fourth Gospel and the Historical Jesus" (pp. 98–113); H. D. Betz, "Jesus as Divine Man" (pp. 114–33); and J. M. Robinson, "Jesus' Parables as God Happening" (pp. 134–50; see #264).

84   C. C. Anderson. *Critical Quests of Jesus.* Grand Rapids: Eerdmans, 1969.

Reviews the major contributions to the scholarly quest of the historical Jesus; argues that gospel accounts are historically reliable.

85   H. Braun. *Jesus of Nazareth: The Man and His Time.* Translated by E. R. Kalin. Philadelphia: Fortress, 1979. Original title: *Jesus: Der Mann aus Nazareth und seine Zeit.* Stuttgart: Kreuz, 1969. Second edition: 1984. Third edition: Gütersloh: Mohn, 1988.

Argues that the essence of Jesus' authority is seen in his emphasis on love and grace, which means accepting one's neighbor and accepting oneself; concludes that the resurrection was not an "event in space and time."

86 H. K. McArthur. *In Search of the Historical Jesus*. New York: Scribner, 1969/London: SPCK, 1970.

A selection of excerpts from leading scholars.

87 G. Strecker. "The Historical and Theological Problem of the Jesus Question." Translated by N. R. Parker. *Toronto Journal of Theology* 6 (1990) 201–23. Original title: "Die historische und theologische Problematik der Jesusfrage." *Evangelische Theologie* 20 (1969) 453–76. Reprinted in Strecker's *Eschaton und Historie*, pp. 159–82. Göttingen: Vandenhoeck & Ruprecht, 1979.

Beginning with M. Kähler's work, reviews four principal approaches (or conceptions) to the problem, concluding that historical findings can never replace the New Testament witness that Jesus is the Christ of faith.

88 W. O. Walker. "The Quest for the Historical Jesus: A Discussion of Methodology." *Anglican Theological Review* 51 (1969) 38–56.

After reviewing authenticity criteria, argues that a picture of the historical Jesus must place Jesus in first-century Palestinian context, explain his Roman execution, and account for the rise of Christianity.

89 O. Cullmann. *Jesus and the Revolutionaries*. Translated by G. Putnam. New York: Harper & Row, 1970. Original title: *Jesus und die Revolutionären seiner Zeit*. Tübingen: Mohr, 1970.

Argues that in his actions and preaching Jesus brings in a new kingdom, but he does not call for violence; concludes that Jesus is in some ways more radical than the zealots, less so in other ways.

90 H. K. McArthur. "The Burden of Proof in Historical Jesus Research." *ExpTim* 82 (1970–71) 116–19.

Argues (pp. 117–18) that the burden of proof initially rests upon those who claim authenticity, but if material has multiple attestation, then the burden shifts to those who deny authenticity.

91   M. Hengel. "Kerygma oder Geschichte? Zur Problematik einer falschen Alternative in der neutestamentlichen Forschung aufgezeigt an Hand einiger neuer Monographien." *Theologische Quartalschrift* 151 (1971) 323–36.
Criticizes the widespread assumption that kerygmatic interests necessarily preclude historically reliable tradition.

92   É. Trocmé. *Jesus and His Contemporaries.* Translated by R. A. Wilson. Philadelphia: Fortress/London: SCM, 1973. Original title: *Jésus de Nazareth vu par les témoins de sa vie.* Bibliothéque Théologique. Neuchâtel: Delachaux & Niestlé, 1971.
A critical evaluation of attempts to write a biography of Jesus; proposes steps that must be taken to avoid error. Concludes that a biography of Jesus is not possible, but we can recover the impression that he made on his contemporaries.

93   C. C. Anderson. *The Historical Jesus: A Continuing Quest.* Grand Rapids: Eerdmans, 1972.
A critical assessment of R. Bultmann and the new quest.

94   J. Bowker. *Jesus and the Pharisees.* New York: Cambridge University Press, 1973.
Argues that Jesus offended virtually all groups and was condemned by the Sanhedrin as a "rebellious elder."

95   G. Vermes. *Jesus the Jew: A Historian's Reading of the Gospels.* New York: Macmillan/London: Collins, 1973. Second edition: 1983.
Extensive use of early Palestinian sources; concludes that Jesus is a *hasid* and so is part of charismatic Judaism.

96   G. Bornkamm. "Jesus Christ." Pp. 145–55 in *New Encyclopaedia Britannica*, vol. 10. Chicago: Encyclopaedia Britannica, 1974 (bibliography by M. J. Suggs).
Concise statement from the new-quest perspective.

97   E. Schillebeeckx. *Jesus: An Experiment in Christology.* Translated by H. Hoskins. New York: Seabury/London: Collins, 1979. Reprinted New York: Crossroad, 1981. Original title: *Jezus: Het verhaal van een levende*. Bloemendaal: Nelissen, 1974. German translation: *Jesus: Die Geschichte von einem Lebenden*. Translated by H. Hoskins. Freiburg: Herder, 1975.

Discussion of historical Jesus on pp. 41–397; claims that behind the church's proclamation is "the concrete person Jesus of Nazareth," which is "the one and only basis for an authentic christology" (p. 82); understands Jesus as a leader of a liberation movement, who offered himself as a servant and who remained silent when condemned in Jerusalem.

98   G. N. Stanton. *Jesus of Nazareth in New Testament Preaching*. SNTSMS 27. Cambridge: Cambridge University Press, 1974.

Argues that there is ample evidence in the New Testament that the early church was interested in the Jesus of history.

99   G. Strecker (ed.). *Jesus Christus in Historie und Theologie: Neutestamentliche Festschrift für Hans Conzelmann zum 60. Geburtstag*. Tübingen: Mohr, 1975.

The first half of the volume (pp. 3–263) is concerned with the historical Jesus. Some of these essays include S. Schulz, "Der historische Jesus: Bilanz der Fragen und Lösungen" (pp. 3–25); A. Lindemann, "Jesus in der Theologie des Neuen Testaments" (pp. 27–58); W. Schmithals, "Jesus und die Apokalyptik" (pp. 59–86); J. Becker, "Das Gottesbild Jesu und die älteste Auslegung von Ostern" (pp. 105–26); H. Thyen, "Der irdische Jesus und die Kirche" (pp. 127–42); and J. Roloff, "Der mitleidende Hohepriester: Zur Frage nach der Bedeutung des irdischen Jesus für die Christologie des Hebräerbriefes" (pp. 143–66).

100 N. A. Dahl. *Jesus in the Memory of the Early Church*. Minneapolis: Augsburg, 1976.

Views the Gospels as testimonies to Jesus' life and work.

101 H. W. Hoehner. *Chronological Aspects of the Life of Christ*. Grand Rapids: Zondervan, 1977.

Series of studies previously published; argues that Jesus' birth was during the winter of 5–4 B.C.E., that Jesus began his ministry in the spring or summer of 29 C.E., and that he was crucified near Passover in 33 C.E.

102 I. H. Marshall. *I Believe in the Historical Jesus*. London: Hodder & Stoughton, 1977.

Argues that although the evangelists interpret the tradition, the essential historicity of the tradition is preserved.

103 C. F. D. Moule. *The Origin of Christology*. Cambridge: Cambridge University Press, 1977.

Argues that New Testament Christology emerged from the teaching and ministry of the historical Jesus, as well as from the Easter experience of the disciples.

104 E. F. Harrison. "Current Thinking about the Life of Jesus." Pp. 63–74 in *Evangelical Roots: A Tribute to Wilbur Smith*. Edited by K. S. Kantzer. Nashville: Nelson, 1978.

Discussion of major contributors and trends in historical-Jesus research.

105 R. Latourelle. *Finding Jesus through the Gospels: History and Hermeneutics*. Translated by A. Owen. New York: Alba, 1979. Original title: *L'accès à Jésus par les Évangiles*. Tournai: Desclée, 1978.

Believes historical Jesus can be found, if one is able to discern the presence of Christian influence.

106 B. F. Meyer. *The Aims of Jesus*. London: SCM, 1979.

Offers trenchant criticism of new quest; places emphasis on Jesus' intentions: out of his love for others Jesus was willing to die in his attempt to restore Israel.

107 J. I. H. McDonald. "The New Quest—Dead End: So What about the Historical Jesus?" Pp. 151–70 in *Studia Biblica 1978*, vol. 2: *Papers on the Gospels*. Edited by E. Livingstone. Sheffield: JSOT Press, 1980.

After discussing the shortcomings of the new quest, proposes moving on with the quest by plotting religious movements, religious roles, and religious symbols in Jesus' time; concludes that the quest is an inescapable part of New Testament theology.

108 J. K. Riches. *Jesus and the Transformation of Judaism*. London: Darton, Longman & Todd, 1980.

Argues that Jesus adapted and reinterpreted many of the most important facets of first-century Judaism.

109 R. T. France and D. Wenham (eds.). *Studies of History and Tradition in the Gospels*. Gospel Perspectives 2. Sheffield: JSOT Press, 1981.

Ten essays, a few of which are particularly relevant for historical-Jesus research, including those by R. J. Banks, "Setting 'the Quest for the Historical Jesus' in a Broader Framework" (pp. 61–82); D. A. Carson, "Historical Tradition in the Fourth Gospel: After Dodd, What?" (pp. 83–146); B. D. Chilton, "Announcement in *Nazara*: An Analysis of Luke 4:16–21" (pp. 147–72); W. L. Craig, "The Empty Tomb of Jesus" (pp. 173–200; see #449); R. T. France, "Scripture, Tradition and History in the Infancy Narratives of Matthew" (pp. 239–66); and P. B. Payne, "The Authenticity of the Parables of Jesus" (pp. 329–44). See also #185.

110 R. A. Guelich. "The Gospels: Portraits of Jesus and His Ministry." *JETS* 24 (1981) 117–25.

Observes with approval the recent tendency among conservatives to view the Gospels as "portraits" of Jesus, rather than as historical records (as in precritical times) or as nonhistorical theological writings (as in skeptical scholarship).

111 D. A. Hagner. "Interpreting the Gospels: The Landscape and the Quest." *JETS* 24 (1981) 23–37.

Argues that, because the incarnation is historical, historical criticism is necessary.

112 R. Riesner. *Jesus als Lehrer: Ein Untersuchung zum Ursprung der Evangelien-Überlieferung*. WUNT 2/7. Tübingen: Mohr, 1981. Third edition: 1988.

Critical of the assumptions and skepticism of form criticism. Argues that the Jesus traditions were preserved by a band of disciples (a "school of Jesus") like other rabbis gathered around themselves; although similar to his contemporaries in many ways, Jesus' expressions of authority stand out as unique. See also Riesner's "Der Ursprung der Jesus-Überlieferung," *Theologische Zeitschrift* 38 (1982) 493–513.

113 R. H. Stein. "'Authentic' or 'Authoritative': What Is the Difference?" *JETS* 24 (1981) 127–30.

Criticizes J. M. Robinson's definition of "authentic" (#59).

114 W. R. Farmer. *Jesus and the Gospel: Tradition, Scripture, and Canon.* Philadelphia: Fortress, 1982.

Believes that we may be optimistic about historical-Jesus research: "We have access to a large body of first-rate historical evidence that is decisive in answering important questions about Jesus" (p. 21).

115 A. E. Harvey. *Jesus and the Constraints of History.* Philadelphia: Westminster/London: Duckworth, 1982.

Although critical, a more positive assessment of what can be known about Jesus. See the review articles by A. N. Sherwin-White, J. D. G. Dunn, and E. P. Sanders in *JSNT* 17 (1983) 4–24.

116 J. D. Crossan. *In Fragments: The Aphorisms of Jesus.* San Francisco: Harper & Row, 1983.

A form-critical analysis of Jesus' aphorisms in the Gospels and in noncanonical sources; believes that in many instances the *ipsissima structura*, though not necessarily the *ipsissima verba*, of the aphorisms have been preserved.

117 F. Hahn. *Historical Investigation and New Testament Faith.* Translated by R. Maddox. Edited by E. Krentz. Philadelphia: Fortress, 1983.

An English translation of two previous studies: "Probleme historischer Kritik," *Zeitschrift für die neutestamentliche Wissenschaft* 63 (1972) 1–17, and "Methodologische Überlegungen zur Rückfrage nach Jesus," in *Rückfrage nach Jesus: Zur Methodik und Bedeutung der Frage nach dem historischen Jesus* (ed. K. Kertelge; Quaestiones Disputatae 63; Freiburg im Breisgau/Basel: Herder, 1974), pp. 11–77. Criticizes the methodology of the new quest; suggests a new way of viewing the faith perspective of the New Testament writings.

118 M. Hengel. *Between Jesus and Paul: Studies in the Earliest History of Christianity*. Translated by J. S. Bowden. Philadelphia: Fortress/London: SCM, 1983.

Argues that Jesus saw himself as Israel's Messiah and believed that his ministry signaled the inauguration of the kingdom of God.

119 E. P. Sanders. "The Search for Bedrock in the Jesus Material." *Proceedings of the Irish Biblical Association* 7 (1983) 74–86.

Concludes that the authentic core of sayings is so small it is necessary to turn to Jesus' actions, particularly with respect to the temple, to begin a reconstruction of the historical Jesus.

120 G. S. Sloyan. *Jesus in Focus: A Life in Its Setting*. Mystic, Conn.: Twenty-Third Publications, 1983.

Emphasizes the first-century Palestinian setting.

121 J. M. Robinson. "The Sayings of Jesus: Q." *Drew Gateway* 54 (1983–84) 26–38.

Argues that "Papyrus Q" takes us closer to the historical Jesus than any other source and notes that it is concerned primarily with action, not theology.

122 E. Bammel and C. F. D. Moule (eds.). *Jesus and the Politics of His Day*. Cambridge: Cambridge University Press, 1984.

Twenty-six studies discussing the question of Jesus' involvement with zealots; contributors include S. G. F. Brandon, B. Reicke, M. Black, W. Grundmann, and others.

123 M. J. Borg. *Conflict, Holiness and Politics in the Teachings of Jesus*. Studies in the Bible and Early Christianity 5. New York/Toronto: Mellen, 1984.

Argues that Jesus' ministry was one of conflict with competing groups claiming to know the way to achieve holiness and national renewal. Contrary to these groups, which emphasized holiness, Jesus emphasized compassion. Consequently he welcomed sinners and outcasts and criticized the exclusive views of others. For a popular version see Borg's *Jesus: A New Vision* (San Francisco: Harper & Row, 1987). See the review by D. M. Smith in *Forum* 5/4 (1989) 71–82.

124 R. H. Fuller. "The Historical Jesus: Some Outstanding Issues." *Thomist* 48 (1984) 368–82.

Interacting with E. Schillebeeckx (#97), examines the question of the relevance of the historical Jesus for Christology, the criteria of authenticity, and the content of Jesus' teaching.

125 E. Grässer. "Norman Perrin's Contribution to the Question of the Historical Jesus." *JR* 64 (1984) 484–500.

Argues that Perrin's contribution lies in his establishing a middle ground between the positions of R. Bultmann and J. Jeremias.

126 D. A. Hagner. *The Jewish Reclamation of Jesus: An Analysis and Critique of Modern Jewish Study of Jesus*. Grand Rapids: Zondervan, 1984.

Discusses Jewish interpretation of Jesus and the law, kingdom of God, righteousness, and Jesus' mission. Provides a good bibliography of Jewish works on Jesus and Christianity.

127 G. Vermes. *Jesus and the World of Judaism*. Philadelphia: Fortress/London: SCM, 1984.

A collection of ten previously published essays, intended as a sequel to his earlier study (#95). Jesus is viewed as a *hasid* of first-century Palestine, since he is presented as a wise teacher, healer, and exorcist.

128 F. F. Bruce. *Jesus: Lord and Savior*. The Jesus Library. Downers Grove, Ill.: InterVarsity, 1986. British edition: *The Real Jesus: Who Is He?* London: Hodder & Stoughton, 1985.

Examines evidence for Jesus, historical setting, basic teaching, ministry, and self-understanding.

129 C. E. Carlston. "Jesus Christ." Pp. 475–87 in *Harper's Dictionary of the Bible*. Edited by P. J. Achtemeier. San Francisco: Harper & Row, 1985.

Provides an assessment and summary of the current scholarly position.

130 J. H. Charlesworth. "Research on the Historical Jesus Today: Jesus and the Pseudepigrapha, the Dead Sea Scrolls, the Nag

Hammadi Codices, Josephus, and Archaeology." *Princeton Seminary Bulletin* 6 (1985) 98–115.

Raises the question in what ways various noncanonical sources contribute to historical-Jesus research.

131 J. D. G. Dunn. *The Evidence for Jesus*. Philadelphia: Westminster/London: SCM, 1985.

Argues that critical scholarship has certainly affected the way that the Gospels are viewed, undermining traditional beliefs, but scholarship has not destroyed their reliability.

132 E. P. Sanders. *Jesus and Judaism*. Philadelphia: Fortress/London: SCM, 1985.

Argues that Jesus was part of Jewish restoration theology. He did not preach repentance (as the Baptist had); he died because he threatened to destroy the temple and build a new one in its place. See the reviews by A. J. Droge in *Criterion* 26 (1987) 15–18 and by D. M. Smith in *Forum* 5/4 (1989) 71–82.

133 D. Oakman. *Jesus and the Economic Questions of His Day*. Studies in the Bible and Early Christianity 8. Lewiston/Queenston: Mellen, 1986.

Considers the significance of first-century Palestinian economics for understanding Jesus' ministry.

134 N. T. Wright. "'Constraints' and the Jesus of History." *SJT* 39 (1986) 189–210.

Responding to A. E. Harvey's *Jesus and the Constraints of History* (#115), criticizes Harvey's understanding of "constraints," especially his understanding of the constraint of Jewish monotheism and early Christology.

135 D. C. Allison Jr. "Jesus and the Covenant: A Response to E. P. Sanders." *JSNT* 29 (1987) 57–78.

Arguing against E. P. Sanders's *Jesus and Judaism* (#132), concludes that Jesus rejected covenantal nomism.

136 R. A. Horsley. *Jesus and the Spiral of Violence: Popular Jewish Resistance in Roman Palestine*. San Francisco/London: Harper & Row, 1987.

Concludes that Jesus was opposed to violence (though not a pacifist), calling for social revolution and an end to oppression. For a further statement see Horsley's article in *Forum* 5/4 (1989) 3–17. For a review see D. E. Smith in *Forum* 5/4 (1989) 18–26.

137 M. J. Borg. "A Renaissance in Jesus Studies." *Theology Today* 45 (1988) 280–92.

Surveys the diverse evidence of a resurgent and widespread interest in Jesus research.

138 J. H. Charlesworth. *Jesus within Judaism*. Anchor Bible Reference Library. New York/London: Doubleday, 1988.

Examines several ancient literatures and aspects of archeology, concluding that there is a new mood of optimism with regard to Jesus research.

139 C. E. B. Cranfield. "Some Reflections on the Subject of the Virgin Birth." *SJT* 41 (1988) 177–89.

Because Messiah was not expected to be born of a virgin, the widespread belief in Jesus' virginal conception must have some basis in history.

140 C. A. Evans. "The Historical Jesus and Christian Faith: A Critical Assessment of a Scholarly Problem." *Christian Scholars Review* 18 (1988) 48–63.

After reviewing major contributions to historical-Jesus research, concludes that although similar errors are being repeated, a new phase seems to be emerging.

141 J. M. Robinson. "The Study of the Historical Jesus after Nag Hammadi." *Semeia* 44 (1988) 45–55.

Argues that the Gnostic materials from Nag Hammadi have broadened the context against which the Synoptic Gospels and the historical Jesus must be studied.

142 P. Stuhlmacher. *Jesus von Nazareth—Christus des Glaubens*. Stuttgart: Calwer, 1988.

Explores the problem of how Jesus' preaching gives way to faith in Jesus as Christ.

143 S. Fowl. "Reconstructing and Deconstructing the Quest of the Historical Jesus." *SJT* 42 (1989) 319–33.

Examining E. P. Sanders's *Jesus and Judaism* (#132), concludes that this book is not part of the quest, since the quest looks for Jesus' personality and self-consciousness.

144 P. Hollenbach. "The Historical Jesus Quest in North America Today." *Biblical Theology Bulletin* 19 (1989) 11–22.

Reviews work (such as that by M. J. Borg [#123], D. Oakman [#133], and R. A. Horsley [#136, #145]) that has broken away from research guided by theological and philosophical interests.

145 R. A. Horsley. *Sociology and the Jesus Movement.* New York: Crossroad, 1989.

Interacting with G. Theissen, argues for a model that more accurately takes into account the political and social factors of first-century Palestine.

146 E. Hurth. *In His Name: Comparative Studies in the Quest for the Historical Jesus.* Frankfurt: Lang, 1989.

Compares the methods and results of German and American scholarship.

147 G. N. Stanton. *The Gospels and Jesus.* Oxford: Oxford University Press, 1989.

Half of the book (pp. 140–273) is devoted to major areas of historical-Jesus study, for example, the evidence for Jesus, John the Baptist, Jesus as prophet, parables, miracles, opposition, and crucifixion.

148 H. C. Kee. *What Can We Know about Jesus?* Understanding Jesus Today. New York/Cambridge: Cambridge University Press, 1990.

Concludes that the ancient evidence provides much helpful information about Jesus.

149 J. P. Meier. "The Historical Jesus: Rethinking Some Concepts." *Theological Studies* 51 (1990) 3–24.

Argues that the distinction between *historisch* and *geschichtlich* ought to be dropped, since the Christ of faith can never be identified with the Jesus of history. The latter guards against subjective interpretations of the former.

150 J. D. Crossan. *The Historical Jesus: The Life of a Mediterranean Jewish Peasant.* San Francisco: Harper & Row/London: Collins, 1991.

Concludes that "the historical Jesus was, then, a *peasant Jewish Cynic.* His peasant village was close enough to a

Greco-Roman city like Sepphoris that sight and knowledge of Cynicism are neither inexplicable nor unlikely" (p.
421, Crossan's emphasis).

151 M. de Jonge. *Jesus, the Servant Messiah*. New Haven/Lon-
don: Yale University Press, 1991.
The 1989 Shaffer Lectures, concludes that Jesus proclaimed the kingdom, thought of himself as the inaugura-
tor of the kingdom, and "regarded himself as the Messiah
and Son of David inspired and empowered by the Spirit"
(p. 75). See also de Jonge's *Christology in Context: The
Earliest Christian Response to Jesus* (Philadelphia: Westminster, 1988).

152 J. P. Meier. *A Marginal Jew: Rethinking the Historical Jesus*,
vol. 1: *The Roots of the Problem and the Person*. Anchor Bible Reference Library. New York/London: Doubleday, 1991.
The first volume of what promises to be a work of major
significance treating sources, authenticity, and the context (social, economic, linguistic, personal) and chronology of Jesus' life. The second volume will treat Jesus' public ministry.

4

Demythologization

Although D. F. Strauss's mythological interpretation of the Gospels was strongly resisted throughout the nineteenth century, theologians in the twentieth century finally came to recognize the problem of mythology and so sought ways to deal with it. The older liberal approach had been to peel it away, in the search for the kernel of the gospel. But R. Bultmann and his followers argued that myth was to be interpreted, not eliminated. G. Bornkamm provides one of the most helpful studies on myth and the gospel (see #156). It is interesting to observe, however, that in recent years the problem of myth, or at least its discussion, has virtually dropped out of the historical-Jesus debate. In some of the most recent and influential studies, it is hardly referred to at all (e.g., G. Vermes [#95, #127], M. J. Borg [#123], E. P. Sanders [#132], and J. P. Meier [#152]).

153 M. Goguel. *Jesus the Nazarene: Myth or History?* Translated by F. Stephens. New York: Appleton/London: Unwin, 1926. Original title: *Jésus de Nazareth, Mythe ou Histoire?* Paris: Payot, 1925.

Although dated, this study is very useful; criticizes the various arguments that Jesus' life is mythical (either that he did not exist or that the Gospels cannot give us accurate knowledge of his life and ministry); concludes that "the historical reality of the personality of Jesus alone enables us to understand the birth and development of

Christianity, which otherwise would remain an enigma" (p. 316). For a history of the "Christ myth" debate see pp. 1–28.

154 R. Bultmann. "New Testament and Mythology." Pp. 1–44 in *Kerygma and Myth: A Theological Debate.* Edited by H.-W. Bartsch. Translated by R. H. Fuller. London: SPCK, 1957. Second edition: 1964. Original title: "Neues Testament und Mythologie." Part 2 of Bultmann's *Offenbarung und Heilsgeschehen.* Beiträge zur evangelischen Theologie 7. Munich: Kaiser, 1941. Reprinted in *Kerygma und Mythos: Ein theologisches Gespräch* [#155], pp. 15–53. Edited by H.-W. Bartsch. Theologische Forschung 1. Hamburg-Bergstedt: Reich & Heidrich, 1948. Fourth edition: 1960. Reprinted as *Neues Testament und Mythologie: Das Problem der Entmythologisierung der neutestamentlichen Verkündigung.* Edited by E. Jüngel. Beiträge zur evangelischen Theologie 96. Munich: Kaiser, 1985.

Classic essay in which it is proposed that the New Testament needs to be "demythologized."

155 H.-W. Bartsch (ed.). *Kerygma and Myth: A Theological Debate.* Translated by R. H. Fuller. London: SPCK, 1957. Second edition: 1964. Original title: *Kerygma und Mythos: Ein theologisches Gespräche.* Theologische Forschung 1. Hamburg-Bergstedt: Reich & Heidrich, 1948. Fourth edition: 1960.

Essays by R. Bultmann, "New Testament and Mythology" (see #154); E. Lohmeyer, "The Right Interpretation of the Mythological" (pp. 124–37); and F. K. Schumann, "Can the Event of Jesus Christ Be Demythologized?" (pp. 175–90). Probably the most frequently cited volume in the years of demythologizing debate that followed. This volume was to become the first of nine entitled *Kerygma und Mythos,* published between 1948 and 1978.

156 G. Bornkamm. "Myth and Gospel: A Discussion of Demythologizing the New Testament Message." Pp. 172–96 in *Kerygma and History: A Symposium on the Theology of Rudolf Bultmann.* Edited and translated by C. E. Braaten and R. A. Harrisville. Nashville: Abingdon, 1962. Original title:

"Evangelium und Mythos: Zur Diskussion des Problemes der Entmythologisierung der neutestamentlichen Verkündigung." *Zeichen der Zeit* 5 (1951) 1–15. Reprinted as "Mythos und Evangelium: Zur Diskussion des Problemes der Entmythologisierung der neutestamentlichen Verkündigung." Pp. 3–29 in *Mythos and Evangelium: Zur Programm R. Bultmanns*. Edited by G. Bornkamm and W. Klaas. Theologische Existenz Heute 26. Munich: Kaiser, 1951. Third edition: 1953.

A critical assessment of R. Bultmann's understanding of demythologizing the Gospels (#154).

157 H.-W. Bartsch (ed.). *Kerygma und Mythos*, vol. 2. Hamburg: Reich, 1952.

Major contributions include those by E. Stauffer, "Entmythologisierung oder Realtheologie?" (pp. 13–28); H. Sauter, "Für und wider Entmythologisierung des Neuen Testamentes" (pp. 41–65); W. G. Kümmel, "Mythische Rede und Heilsgeschehen im Neuen Testament" (pp. 153–69; reprinted in Kümmel's *Heilsgeschehen und Geschichte* [ed. E. Grässer et al.; Marburg: Elwert, 1965], pp. 153–68); and R. Bultmann, "Zum Problem der Entmythologisierung" (pp. 177–208; English translation: "On the Problem of Demythologization" in #165).

158 F. Gogarten. *Demythologizing and History*. Translated by N. H. Smith. New York: Scribner, 1955. Original title: *Entmythologisierung und Kirche*. Stuttgart: Vorwerk, 1953. Fourth edition: 1966.

Discusses R. Bultmann's demythologizing hermeneutic (#154) and tries to explain its relationship to history; defends Bultmann against the charge that he has denied the historicity of Christianity; and concludes that the church can no longer return to the creeds of the past.

159 E. Fuchs. *Das Programm der Entmythologisierung*. Bad Cannstatt: Müllerschön, 1954. Third edition: 1967.

Discusses R. Bultmann's demythologizing hermeneutic (#154) and works out what he thinks is the proper application. See also Fuchs's *Hermeneutik* (2d ed.; Bad Cannstatt: Müllerschön, 1958).

160 C. K. Barrett. "Myth and the New Testament: The Greek Word μῦθος." *ExpTim* 68 (1956–57) 345–48.

Argues that myth is a medium by which theological and philosophical truth is articulated; but the New Testament repudiates the kind of myth that is invented (or newly created) in the sense of falsehoods.

161 C. K. Barrett. "Myth and the New Testament: How Far Does Myth Enter into the New Testament?" *ExpTim* 68 (1956–57) 359–62.

Explains that myth utilizes supernatural beings in telling a narrative; therefore, much of the New Testament is mythical, and much of this myth has been mediated through Jewish apocalyptic.

162 R. Bultmann. *Jesus Christ and Mythology.* New York: Scribner/London: SCM, 1958. Reprinted 1966.

Brief description of mythology in the New Testament, the beginnings of demythologization of eschatology in the New Testament, and the modern expression of a demythologized Christian message.

163 J. M. Robinson. "New Testament Faith Today." *Journal of Bible and Religion* 27 (1959) 233–42.

Defines the meaning of faith in the context of demythologized gospel and existentialism.

164 R. Bultmann. "A Chapter in the Problem of Demythologizing." Pp. 1–9 in *New Testament Sidelights: Essays in Honor of Alexander Converse Purdy.* Edited by H. K. McArthur. Hartford, Conn.: Hartford Seminary Foundation, 1960.

Makes it clear that it is the New Testament's world view that is demythologized, not its thoughts, as some have misunderstood Bultmann to mean; argues that to speak of God, we can only speak of his work in us, in our existence.

165 R. Bultmann. "On the Problem of Demythologizing." *JR* 42 (1962) 96–102. Reprinted in *New Testament Issues*, pp. 35–44. Edited by R. Batey. New York: Harper & Row, 1970. Original title: "Zum Problem der Entmythologisierung." Pp. 19–26 in *Il problema della demitizzazione* (accompanied by an Italian translation, pp. 27–34). Edited by E. Castelli. Rome: Archivio di Filosofia, 1961.

Explains Bultmann's understanding of the relationship of demythologization to history.

166 C. E. Braaten and R. A. Harrisville (eds.). *Kerygma and History: A Symposium on the Theology of Rudolf Bultmann.* Nashville: Abingdon, 1962.
Contains articles concerned with mythology by C. E. Braaten, E. Ellwein, E. Kinder, W. Künneth, R. Prenter, and G. Bornkamm (#156).

167 N. Perrin. *The Promise of Bultmann.* The Promise of Theology. Philadelphia/New York: Lippincott, 1969.
Provides a lucid summary and assessment of R. Bultmann's understanding of history, faith, demythologization, etc.

168 J. D. G. Dunn. "Demythologizing—the Problem of Myth in the New Testament." Pp. 285–307 in *New Testament Interpretation: Essays on Principles and Methods.* Edited by I. H. Marshall. Grand Rapids: Eerdmans/Exeter: Paternoster, 1977.
Assesses the understanding of myth in D. F. Strauss (#38) and R. Bultmann (#154); criticizes Bultmann's definition of myth, which he (Bultmann) believes makes it impossible to talk of God.

169 R. Bultmann. *New Testament and Mythology and Other Basic Writings.* Translated and edited by S. M. Ogden. Philadelphia: Fortress, 1984/London: SCM, 1985.
An English translation of a selection of Bultmann's writings.

170 U. Luz. "Rückkehr des mythologischen Weltbildes: Überlegungen bei einer neuen Lektüre von Bultmanns Programm der Entmythologisierung." *Reformatio* 33 (1984) 448–53.
Looking back to R. Bultmann's seminal study in 1941 (#154), ponders the future of demythologization.

5

Authenticity Criteria

With the rise of form criticism, the critical disposition toward the historical reliability of the gospel tradition became much more skeptical. In the minds of many, the burden of proof rests upon the claim to authenticity. In any case, several criteria have been proposed and utilized for establishing authentic material in the gospel tradition. In §5.1 general studies are listed that discuss the problem of authenticity and the various criteria that have been proposed. In §5.2–§5.11 the individual criteria themselves are described and documented (the bibliographic entries listed in each of these sections contain further examples of the criterion under discussion).

5.1 General Bibliography

171 F. C. Grant. "The Authenticity of Jesus' Sayings." Pp. 137–43 in *Neutestamentliche Studien für Rudolf Bultmann zu seinen siebzigsten Geburtstag.* Edited by W. Eltester. Beihefte zur Zeitschrift für die neutestamentliche Wissenschaft 21. Berlin: Töpelmann, 1954.

Makes useful distinctions in the degrees of authenticity.

172 H. K. McArthur. "A Survey of Recent Gospel Research." *Interp* 18 (1964) 39–55 (esp. 47–51).

173 R. H. Fuller. *A Critical Introduction to the New Testament,* pp. 94–98. London: Duckworth, 1966.

174 N. Perrin. *Rediscovering the Teaching of Jesus*, pp. 15–53. New York: Harper & Row, 1967.

Discusses the criteria of dissimilarity and coherence.

175 W. O. Walker. "The Quest for the Historical Jesus: A Discussion of Methodology." *Anglican Theological Review* 51 (1969) 38–56.

Very helpful discussion; assesses several of the criteria of authenticity.

176 M. Lehmann. *Synoptische Quellensanalyse und die Frage nach dem historischen Jesus*, pp. 163–205. Beihefte zur Zeitschrift für die neutestamentliche Wissenschaft 38. Berlin: Töpelmann, 1970.

Examines the synoptic materials as sources for the historical Jesus and how to determine their authenticity.

177 H. K. McArthur. "The Burden of Proof in Historical Jesus Research." *ExpTim* 82 (1970–71) 116–19.

Argues (pp. 117–18) that the burden of proof initially rests upon those who claim authenticity, but if material has multiple attestation, then the burden shifts to those who deny authenticity.

178 M. D. Hooker. "Christology and Methodology." *NTS* 17 (1970–71) 480–87.

Criticizes the weaknesses of the criteria of dissimilarity and coherence.

179 R. S. Barbour. *Traditio-Historical Criticism of the Gospels*, pp. 1–27. London: SPCK, 1972.

Criticizes the logic and presuppositions of several of the criteria.

180 D. G. A. Calvert. "An Examination of the Criteria for Distinguishing the Authentic Words of Jesus." *NTS* 18 (1971–72) 209–19.

Surveys criteria; suggests that tradition contrary to an evangelist's theological tendency may have claim to authenticity.

181 M. D. Hooker. "On Using the Wrong Tool." *Theology* 75 (1972) 570–81.

Penetrating criticism of some of the criteria.

182 R. Latourelle. "Critères d'authenticité historique des Évangiles." *Gregorianum* 55 (1974) 609–38 (esp. 619–35).

Identifies three categories: (1) basic criteria, (2) dependent criteria, and (3) composite criteria.

183 R. N. Longenecker. "Literary Criteria in Life of Jesus Research: An Evaluation and Proposal." Pp. 217–29 in *Current Issues in Biblical and Patristic Interpretation: Studies in Honor of Merrill C. Tenney*. Edited by G. F. Hawthorne. Grand Rapids: Eerdmans, 1975.

Surveys criteria; follows up on D. G. A. Calvert's suggestion (#180) that material contrary to theological orientation of the evangelist may reflect early, widely respected, and perhaps authentic tradition.

184 R. T. France. "The Authenticity of the Sayings of Jesus." Pp. 101–43 in *History, Criticism, and Faith*. Edited by C. Brown. Downers Grove, Ill.: InterVarsity, 1976.

A survey and assessment of criteria.

185 R. H. Stein. "The 'Criteria' for Authenticity." Pp. 225–63 in *Studies of History and Tradition in the Four Gospels*. Edited by R. T. France and D. Wenham. Gospel Perspectives 2. Sheffield: JSOT Press, 1980.

Best survey of the criteria to date.

186 S. C. Goetz and C. L. Blomberg. "The Burden of Proof." *JSNT* 11 (1981) 39–63.

Argues that the burden of proof rests on those who deny the historical reliability of the Gospels, since the Gospels were written as history.

187 R. H. Stein. "'Authentic' or 'Authoritative'? What Is the Difference?" *JETS* 24 (1981) 127–30.

Criticizes the oft-held idea that what is truly "authentic" is what is authoritative for Christians, whether or not Jesus himself actually said it.

188 A. E. Harvey. *Jesus and the Constraints of History*, pp. 1–10. Philadelphia: Westminster/London: Duckworth, 1982.

Discusses several criteria.

189 M. E. Boring. "Criteria of Authenticity: The Beatitudes as a Test Case." *Forum* 1/4 (1985) 3–38.

190 D. Polkow. "Method and Criteria for Historical Jesus Research." *SBLSP* 26 (1987) 336–56.

Subdivides the authenticity criteria into twenty-five categories and examines the parable of the mustard seed in light of them.

191 J. D. Crossan. "Divine Immediacy and Human Immediacy: Towards a New First Principle in Historical Jesus Research." *Semeia* 44 (1988) 121–40.

Using a unit from Q (Luke 6:29–30 ‖ Matt 5:39b–42; cf. Gospel of Thomas 95), argues for a criteria of authenticity that seeks to uncover the version that best explains the other parallels.

192 J. D. Crossan. "Materials and Methods in Historical Jesus Research." *Forum* 4/4 (1988) 3–24.

Working out several principles and criteria, proposes 107 units as constituting the primary stratum for Jesus research. See further discussion in Crossan's *Historical Jesus* (#150, pp. 427–50).

193 M. J. Borg. "What Did Jesus Really Say?" *Bible Review* 5/5 (1989) 18–25.

Discusses criteria of authenticity; argues that critical scholarship provides access only to the Jesus of history.

194 C. A. Evans. "Authenticity Criteria in Life of Jesus Research." *Christian Scholars Review* 19 (1989) 6–31.

After surveying various criteria and examples, a "refashioned dissimilarity criterion" is proposed: "Material that reflects the social, political, and theological context of Jesus' time, but does not reflect the interests of the church in ways that are inconsistent with those of Jesus, has a reasonable claim to authenticity" (pp. 26–27). The parables of the wicked vineyard tenants (Mark 12:1–11 and parallels) and the prodigal son (Luke 15:11–32) are examined in the light of this proposed criterion.

195 J. P. Meier. *A Marginal Jew: Rethinking the Historical Jesus*, vol. 1: *The Roots of the Problem and the Person*. Anchor Bible Reference Library. New York/London: Doubleday, 1991.

Excellent discussion of criteria on pp. 167–95.

5.2 Multiple Attestation

The claim to authenticity of a given saying is strengthened if it is found in two or more traditions (Mark, Q, M, L). F. C. Burkitt (#196) identified thirty-one such sayings. Since the Coptic Gnostic Gospel of Thomas may contain early, even independent tradition, some scholars use it as well. Examples include the following:

the lamp saying, in Mark (4:21 ‖ Luke 8:16) and Q (Matt 5:15 ‖ Luke 11:33)

the saying on what is hidden, in Mark (4:22 ‖ Luke 8:17), Q (Matt 10:26b ‖ Luke 12:2), and Thomas (5b)

the evil generation saying, in Mark (8:12 ‖ Matt 16:4) and Q (Matt 12:39b ‖ Luke 11:29b)

196 F. C. Burkitt. *The Gospel History and Its Transmission*, pp. 147–66. Edinburgh: T. & T. Clark, 1906. Third edition: 1911.

197 C. H. Dodd. *The Parables of the Kingdom*, p. 20. London: Nisbet, 1935. Second edition: New York: Scribner, 1961.

198 H. K. McArthur. "The Burden of Proof in Historical Jesus Research." *ExpTim* 82 (1970–71) 116–19.

Argues (pp. 117–18) that the burden of proof initially rests upon those who claim authenticity, but if material has multiple attestation, then the burden shifts to those who deny authenticity.

5.3 Multiple Forms

First proposed by C. H. Dodd (#199), the criterion of multiple forms argues that those sayings of Jesus found in two or more forms of tradition (e.g., sayings, parables, stories) represent early and widespread tradition and may well reflect authentic material. Examples include the following:

the coming of the kingdom of God: Matt 5:17; 9:37–38; 13:16–17; Mark 2:18–20; 4:26–29; Luke 11:14–22; John 4:35

Jesus' mercy to sinners: Matt 11:19; Mark 2:15–17; Luke 15:2

Jesus' teaching regarding the Sabbath: Mark 3:1–6; Luke 14:1–6; John 5:9–17; 7:22–24; 9:14–16

199 C. H. Dodd. *History and the Gospel*, pp. 91–101. New York: Scribner, 1937.

200 J. M. Robinson. "The Formal Structure of Jesus' Message." Pp. 91–110 and 273–84 (see pp. 96–97) in *Current Issues in New Testament Interpretation: Essays in Honor of Otto A. Piper*. Edited by W. Klassen and G. F. Snyder. New York: Harper, 1962.

201 H. K. McArthur. "A Survey of Recent Gospel Research." *Interp* 18 (1964) 39–55 (see pp. 49–50).

202 W. O. Walker. "The Quest for the Historical Jesus: A Discussion of Methodology." *Anglican Theological Review* 51 (1969) 38–56 (see pp. 42–43).

203 D. G. A. Calvert. "An Examination of the Criteria for Distinguishing the Authentic Words of Jesus." *NTS* 18 (1971–72) 209–19 (see p. 217).

204 R. H. Stein. "The 'Criteria' for Authenticity." Pp. 225–63 (see pp. 232–33) in *Studies of History and Tradition in the Four Gospels*. Edited by R. T. France and D. Wenham. Gospel Perspectives 2. Sheffield: JSOT Press, 1980.

5.4 Semitic Features and Palestinian Background

It has been argued, or assumed, that the retention of Semitic and Palestinian features in the Greek Gospels points to authenticity, since Jesus' words were originally spoken in Aramaic and in Palestine. However, critics of this criterion point out that the presence of Semitic and Palestinian features may only reflect the early church, which was Palestinian and largely Aramaic-speaking. Examples include the following:

Aramaic words and phrases
　　bar ("son"): Matt 16:17
　　talitha cum ("little girl, arise"): Mark 5:41
　　ephphatha ("be opened"): Mark 7:34
　　golgotha ("skull"): Mark 15:22

eloi eloi lama sabachthani ("My God, my God, why have
you forsaken me?"): Mark 15:34
the "divine passive" and other ways of avoiding the mention of
"God": Matt 5:3–10; 6:9; 13:11; Mark 14:62; Luke 7:35; 17:30
poetic devices: Matt 11:5–6; Mark 9:50; Luke 14:34–35
word play: "straining out a gnat [*qalma*] and swallowing a
camel [*gamla*]": Matt 23:24

205 G. H. Dalman. *The Words of Jesus: Considered in the Light
of Post-Biblical Jewish Writings and the Aramaic language*,
pp. 17–42. Translated by D. M. Kay. Edinburgh: T. & T.
Clark, 1902. Original title: *Die Worte Jesu, mit Berücksichtigung des nachkanonischen jüdischen Schriftums und der
aramäischen Sprache*, vol. 1, esp. pp. 13–34. Leipzig: Hinrichs, 1898. Second edition: 1930.
   A classic study; has served as the point of departure for all
other studies in this field.

206 C. F. Burney. *The Poetry of Our Lord: An Examination of the
Formal Elements of Hebrew Poetry in the Discourse of Jesus
Christ*. Oxford: Clarendon, 1925.

207 C. C. Torrey. *The Four Gospels*. New York: Harper/London:
Hodder & Stoughton, 1933. Reprinted 1947.
   Both the works of C. F. Burney (#206) and Torrey have
been criticized for exaggerating the extent of the Semitic
influence underlying the four Gospels (e.g., that the Gospels may have originally been written in Aramaic or
Hebrew).

208 M. Black. *An Aramaic Approach to the Gospels and Acts*
(esp. pp. 50–185). Oxford: Clarendon, 1946. Third edition:
1967.
   A much more balanced discussion of the presence Semitic
influence in the Gospels.

209 J. Jeremias. *New Testament Theology: The Proclamation of
Jesus*, pp. 3–37. Translated by J. S. Bowden. New York: Scrib-
ner/London: SCM, 1971. Original title: *Neutestamentliche
Theologie*, vol. 1: *Die Verkündigung Jesu* (esp. pp. 14–45).
Gütersloh: Mohn, 1971.

A very readable distillation of the work of previous scholars (esp. #205, #206, #207, #208), with many original and penetrating insights.

210 M. McNamara. *Targum and Testament*, pp. 94–96. Grand Rapids: Eerdmans/Shannon: Irish University Press, 1972.

Many examples of the value of the targumic tradition for New Testament interpretation.

211 B. D. Chilton. *A Galilean Rabbi and His Bible: Jesus' Use of the Interpreted Scripture of His Time*. Good News Studies 8. Wilmington, Del.: Glazier, 1984. British edition: *A Galilean Rabbi and His Bible: Jesus' Own Interpretation of Isaiah*. London: SPCK, 1984.

Shows how targumic diction and theme underlie the dominical tradition; many helpful examples.

5.5 Proleptic Eschatology

J. Weiss (#212) argued years ago that the historical Jesus had a proleptic eschatological understanding, that is, Jesus believed that the world would end soon and that the kingdom of God would dawn. Material that reflects this eschatological outlook, Weiss and others believe, has a strong claim to authenticity. Not all scholars, however, accept this criterion (e.g., M. J. Borg, #123 and #287). Examples include the following:

on the nearness of the kingdom: Matt 4:23; 9:35; Mark 1:15; 8:11; 14:25; Luke 4:43; 8:1

on the coming of the "Son of Man": Matt 24:27, 44; Luke 11:30; 12:40; 17:24, 30

212 J. Weiss. *Jesus' Proclamation of the Kingdom of God*. Translated by R. H. Hiers and D. L. Holland. Lives of Jesus Series. Philadelphia: Fortress, 1971. Reprinted Chico, Calif.: Scholars Press, 1985. Original title: *Die Predigt Jesu vom Reiche Gottes*. Göttingen: Vandenhoeck & Ruprecht, 1892. Second edition: 1900. Third edition edited by F. Hahn; introduction by R. Bultmann: 1964.

Classic statement of the view; runs contrary to then-widespread belief that Jesus' preaching was primarily concerned with social reform.

213 A. Schweitzer. *The Quest of the Historical Jesus: A Critical Study of Its Progress from Reimarus to Wrede.* Translated by W. Montgomery. New York: Macmillan/London: Black, 1910. Reprinted 1954; New York: Macmillan, 1968 (introduction by J. M. Robinson); London: SCM, 1981. Original title: *Von Reimarus zu Wrede: Eine Geschichte des Leben-Jesu-Forschung.* Tübingen: Mohr, 1906. Second edition: *Die Geschichte der Leben-Jesu-Forschung.* Tübingen: Mohr, 1913. Sixth edition: 1951.

Argues for a more consistent application of the criterion of proleptic eschatology; all of Jesus' activity must be seen in the light of this understanding.

214 T. W. Manson. *The Teaching of Jesus*, pp. 244–84. Cambridge: Cambridge University Press, 1931. Second edition: 1935.

215 W. G. Kümmel. *Promise and Fulfillment.* Translated by D. M. Barton. SBT 23. Naperville, Ill.: Allenson/London: SCM, 1957. Original title: *Verheissung und Erfüllung: Untersuchungen zur eschatologischen Verkündigung Jesu*, pp. 47–57. Basel: Majer, 1945. Second edition: Zurich: Zwingli, 1953.

216 R. Bultmann. *Theology of the New Testament*, vol. 1, pp. 3–11. Translated by K. Grobel. New York: Scribner/London: SCM, 1951. Reprinted 1965. Original title: *Theologie des Neuen Testaments*, vol. 1, pp. 2–10. Tübingen: Mohr, 1948. Fifth edition: 1965.

217 R. Schnackenburg. *God's Rule and Kingdom.* Translated by J. Murray. New York: Herder & Herder, 1963. Reprinted London: Burns & Oates, 1968. Original title: *Gottes Herrschaft und Reich: Eine biblisch-theologische Studie*, pp. 135–48. Freiburg: Herder, 1959.

218 J. Jeremias. *New Testament Theology: The Proclamation of Jesus*, pp. 3–37. Translated by J. S. Bowden. New York: Scribner/London: SCM, 1971. Original title: *Neutestamentliche*

Theologie, vol. 1: *Die Verkündigung Jesu*, pp. 101–5. Gütersloh: Mohn, 1971.

219 E. P. Sanders. *Jesus and Judaism*. Philadelphia: Fortress/London: SCM, 1985.

A provocatively fresh and stimulating presentation of Jesus from this perspective. See comments at #132.

5.6 Dissimilarity

The criterion of dissimilarity argues that the only material that may be regarded as having a reasonable claim to authenticity is that which is dissimilar to or distinct from tendencies in Judaism prior to Jesus and tendencies in the church after Jesus. Obviously this criterion, if applied strictly and apart from other criteria, excludes much authentic material. For this and other reasons, the criterion has come under increasing criticism. The parables are considered the most authentic material, for they are distinctive in form and in theme. Examples include the following:

casting out demons by the finger of God: Luke 11:20
the kingdom in the midst of people: Luke 17:20–21
violent entry into the kingdom: Matt 11:12

220 R. Bultmann. *The History of the Synoptic Tradition*, p. 205. Translated by J. Marsh. New York: Harper & Row/Oxford: Blackwell, 1963. Reprinted 1972. Original title: *Die Geschichte der synoptiker Tradition*, p. 222. Forschungen zur Religion und Literatur des Alten und Neuen Testaments 12. Göttingen: Vandenhoeck & Ruprecht, 1921. Second edition: 1931. Third edition: 1958.

Believes that authentic tradition must meet this criterion.

221 E. Käsemann. "The Problem of the Historical Jesus." Pp. 15–47 in Käsemann's *Essays on New Testament Themes*. Translated by W. J. Montague. SBT 41. Naperville, Ill.: Allenson/London: SCM, 1964. Original title: "Das Problem des historischen Jesus." *ZTK* 51 (1954) 125–53. Reprinted in Käsemann's *Exegetische Versuche und Besinnungen*, vol. 1, pp. 187–214. Göttingen: Vandenhoeck & Ruprecht, 1960.

"[Material is authentic] when there are no grounds either for deriving [it] from Judaism or for ascribing it to primitive Christianity" (p. 37). See also comments at #54.

222 J. M. Robinson. *A New Quest of the Historical Jesus*, pp. 116–19. SBT 25. Naperville, Ill.: Allenson/London: SCM, 1959. Reprinted Missoula, Mont.: Scholars Press, 1979. Reprinted as *A New Quest of the Historical Jesus and Other Essays*. Philadelphia: Fortress, 1983. German edition: *Kerygma und historischer Jesus*. Translated by H.-D. Knigge. Zurich/Stuttgart: Zwingli, 1960. Second edition: 1967.

Positive view of the criterion of dissimilarity.

223 R. H. Fuller. *Foundations of New Testament Christology*, p. 18. New York: Scribner/London: Lutterworth, 1965. Reprinted London: Collins, 1969.

224 N. Perrin. *Rediscovering the Teaching of Jesus*, p. 39. New York: Harper & Row, 1967.

Believes that authentic tradition must meet this criterion. Most of the synoptic examples cited above are discussed on pp. 63–77.

225 N. Perrin. *What Is Redaction Criticism?*, p. 71. Guides to Biblical Scholarship. Philadelphia: Fortress, 1969.

226 M. D. Hooker. "On Using the Wrong Tool." *Theology* 75 (1972) 570–81.

See pp. 574–75 for penetrating criticism of the criterion of dissimilarity.

227 R. T. France. "The Authenticity of the Sayings of Jesus." Pp. 101–43 in *History, Criticism, and Faith*. Edited by C. Brown. Downers Grove, Ill.: InterVarsity, 1976.

See pp. 110–14 for criticism of the criterion.

228 D. L. Mealand. "The Dissimilarity Test." *SJT* 31 (1978) 41–50.

Argues that the criterion of dissimilarity is still the best test, but must be used with caution.

229 B. D. Chilton. *A Galilean Rabbi and His Bible: Jesus' Use of the Interpreted Scripture of His Time*. Good News Studies 8. Wilmington, Del.: Glazier, 1984. British edition: *A Galilean*

Rabbi and His Bible: Jesus' Own Interpretation of Isaiah.
London: SPCK, 1984.

See pp. 86–87 for criticism of the criterion of dissimilarity.

230 E. P. Sanders. *Jesus and Judaism.* Philadelphia: Fortress/London: SCM, 1985.

See pp. 16–17 for criticism of the criterion of dissimilarity.

5.7 Least Distinctive

According to R. Bultmann, "whenever narratives pass from mouth to mouth the central point of the narrative and general structure are well preserved; but in the incidental details changes take place, for imagination paints such details with increasing distinctiveness" (#231, p. 345). Consequently, Bultmann and others believe that the least distinctive tradition has the best claim to authenticity. Not all scholars agree, however, for the tendencies of the synoptic tradition have been found not to develop in consistent patterns, as this criterion must presuppose. Assuming that Mark was written first and that Matthew and Luke used it as one of their sources, one should expect greater detail in the later Gospels. Sometimes this is the case (compare Mark 1:4 with Luke 3:2b–3; Mark 1:6 with Matt 3:4), sometimes it is not (compare Mark 1:39 with Luke 4:44; Mark 1:29–30 with Matt 8:14). Obviously the picture becomes even more inconsistent if Matthew or Luke should be viewed as prior.

231 R. Bultmann. "The New Approach to the Synoptic Problem." *JR* 6 (1926) 337–62. Reprinted in Bultmann's *Existence and Faith*, pp. 35–54. New York: Harper & Row, 1960.

232 E. P. Sanders. *The Tendencies of the Synoptic Tradition*, pp. 272–75. SNTSMS 9. Cambridge: Cambridge University Press, 1969.

Sanders observes: "There are no hard and fast laws of the development of the Synoptic tradition. On all counts the tradition developed in opposite directions. It became both longer and shorter, both more and less detailed, and both and more and less Semitic" (p. 272).

233 L. R. Keylock. "Bultmann's Law of Increasing Distinctness." Pp. 193–210 in *Current Issues in Biblical and Patristic Inter-*

pretation: Studies in Honor of Merrill C. Tenney. Edited by
G. F. Hawthorne. Grand Rapids: Eerdmans, 1975.
Critical assessment of Bultmann's position.

5.8 Tradition Contrary to Editorial Tendency

Recently it has been suggested that the presence of tradition
that is clearly contrary to the editorial tendency of the evangelist
has a stronger claim to authenticity. D. G. A. Calvert states:
"The inclusion of material which does not especially serve his
purpose may well be taken as a testimony to the authenticity of
that material, or at least to the inclusion of it in the tradition of
the Church in such a clear and consistent way that the evangelist
was loath to omit it" (#235, p. 219). Examples include the following:

contrary to Mark's negative portrayal of them, in 1:16–18 and
2:14 the disciples respond promptly to Jesus' summons to
discipleship
contrary to his view that the law is of everlasting value (5:17–
20), the Matthean evangelist retains a saying that implies it
has ended with John the Baptist (11:13)

234 C. F. D. Moule. *The Phenomenon of the New Testament*, pp.
56–76. London: SCM, 1967.

235 D. G. A. Calvert. "An Examination of the Criteria for Distinguishing the Authentic Words of Jesus." *NTS* 18 (1971–72)
209–19.

236 R. N. Longenecker. "Literary Criteria in Life of Jesus Research: An Evaluation and Proposal." Pp. 217–29 (see pp.
226–27) in *Current Issues in Biblical and Patristic Interpretation: Studies in Honor of Merrill C. Tenney*. Edited by G. F.
Hawthorne. Grand Rapids: Eerdmans, 1975.

5.9 Prophetic Criticism

Recently J. A. Sanders suggested that the presence of prophetic
criticism may point to authentic tradition. The recovery of such
a prophetic hermeneutic is made through comparative analysis

of the ancient interpretations of Old Testament passages and themes (sometimes called "comparative midrash"). Sanders states: "This method of comparative midrash . . . can be an aid, it seems to me, in piercing back of Luke to Jesus himself" (#238, p. 104). The point that Sanders makes is that what Jesus originally intended as prophetic criticism of his own people later came to be understood statically as criticism of outsiders (i.e., non-Christians) and so was preserved. Examples include the following:

> Jesus' challenge to assumptions about election in his Nazareth sermon (Luke 4:16–30) and in his great banquet parable (Luke 14:15–24) probably reflect this prophetic hermeneutic

237 J. A. Sanders. "The Ethic of Election in Luke's Great Banquet Parable." Pp. 245–271 (esp. pp. 253 and 266) in *Essays in Old Testament Ethics (J. Philip Hyatt, In Memoriam)*. Edited by J. L. Crenshaw and J. T. Willis. New York: Ktav, 1974.

238 J. A. Sanders. "From Isaiah 61 to Luke 4." Pp. 75–106 (esp. pp. 99–101) in *Christianity, Judaism and Other Greco-Roman Cults: Studies for Morton Smith at Sixty*, vol. 1: *New Testament*. Edited by J. Neusner. Studies in Judaism in Late Antiquity 12/1. Leiden: Brill, 1975.

5.10 Contradiction

The criterion of contradiction says that those materials that contradict known environmental conditions of first-century Palestine or that contradict materials that have been established as authentic by means of other criteria should be regarded as inauthentic. Examples include the following:

> the saying about women divorcing their husbands, since apparently Jewish women could do no such thing: Mark 10:12 (this example is not accepted by all)
> the saying about hating one's wife and family (Luke 14:26) may contradict the saying about honoring one's father and mother (Mark 7:9–10)

the prophecy of the temple's destruction may represent a *vaticinium ex eventu*: Mark 13:2

239 D. G. A. Calvert. "An Examination of the Criteria for Distinguishing the Authentic Words of Jesus." *NTS* 18 (1971–72) 209–19 (esp. pp. 212–13).

240 R. H. Stein. "The 'Criteria' for Authenticity." Pp. 225–63 (esp. pp. 248–50) in *Studies of History and Tradition in the Four Gospels*. Edited by R. T. France and D. Wenham. Gospel Perspectives 2. Sheffield: JSOT Press, 1980.

5.11 Consistency (or Coherence)

The consistency criterion is the opposite of the contradiction criterion (§5.10). N. Perrin's statement of the criterion is commonly accepted: "Material which is consistent with, or coheres with, material established as authentic by other means may also be accepted" (#246, p. 71). C. Carlston suggests that such a criterion meet the following two requirements: (1) the saying should "fit reasonably well into the eschatologically based demand for repentance that was characteristic of Jesus' message" (e.g., Mark 1:15; Matt 4:17); and (2) the authentic material should "reflect or fit into the conditions (social, political, ecclesiastical, linguistic, etc.) prevailing during the earthly ministry of Jesus" (#244, p. 34). The best-known examples that receive support from this criterion are the parables. Sayings that cohere with what on other grounds is regarded as authentic include the following (see R. Bultmann, #241):

coherence with Jesus' eschatological orientation: Mark 3:24–27
coherence with demand for repentance: Mark 8:35; 10:23b, 25; Luke 9:60a, 62; Matt 7:13–14
coherence with demand for a new way of thinking: Mark 7:15; 10:15; Luke 14:11; 16:15; Matt 5:39b–41, 44–48

241 R. Bultmann. *The History of the Synoptic Tradition*, p. 105. Translated by J. Marsh. New York: Harper & Row/Oxford: Blackwell, 1963. Reprinted 1972. Original title: *Die Geschichte der synoptiker Tradition*, p. 110. Forschungen zur

Religion und Literatur des Alten und Neuen Testaments 12. Göttingen: Vandenhoeck & Ruprecht, 1921. Second edition: 1931. Third edition: 1958.

242 C. H. Dodd. *The Parables of the Kingdom*. London: Nisbet, 1935. Second edition: New York: Scribner, 1961.
With regard to Jesus' parables, Dodd holds that "certainly there is no part of the Gospel record which has for the reader a clearer ring of authenticity" (p. 1).

243 J. Jeremias. *The Parables of Jesus*, p. 11. Translated by S. H. Hooke. New Testament Library. London: SCM, 1963. Third edition: New York: Scribner, 1972. Original title: *Die Gleichnisse Jesu*. Zurich: Zwingli, 1947. Tenth edition: Göttingen: Vandenhoeck & Ruprecht, 1984.
The parables rest upon "a particularly firm historical foundation" (p. 11).

244 C. E. Carlston. "A *Positive* Criterion of Authenticity?" *Biblical Research* 7 (1962) 33–44.

245 N. Perrin. *Rediscovering the Teaching of Jesus*. New York: Harper & Row, 1967.
On the criterion of coherence see p. 43; on the reliability of parables tradition see pp. 20–22. See #252 below.

246 N. Perrin. *What Is Redaction Criticism?* Guides to Biblical Scholarship. Philadelphia: Fortress, 1969.

247 J. Jeremias. *New Testament Theology: The Proclamation of Jesus*, p. 30. Translated by J. S. Bowden. New York: Scribner/ London: SCM, 1971. Original title: *Neutestamentliche Theologie*, vol. 1: *Die Verkündigung Jesu*, p. 39. Gütersloh: Mohn, 1971.
Argues that in light of the criterion of coherence one may regard the parables as the "bedrock" of the tradition.

6

Teaching of Jesus

Although there are many general studies on the teaching of Jesus, because of the complexities of the problems the subject is divided into several subcategories: general (§6.1), parables (§6.2), the kingdom of God (§6.3), the Sermon on the Mount (and ethics) (§6.4), prayer (§6.5), and the law (§6.6). Jesus' teaching concerning himself is considered in chapter 7.

6.1 General Bibliography

248 C. G. Montefiore. *Rabbinic Literature and Gospel Teachings*. London: Macmillan, 1930. Reprinted New York: Ktav, 1970.

Systematically compares the teachings of Jesus and the Gospels to that of the rabbis.

249 T. W. Manson. *The Teaching of Jesus: Studies of Its Form and Content*. Cambridge: Cambridge University Press, 1931. Second edition: 1935.

Argues that Jesus' teaching is lived out in his life; the kingdom of God was the sphere in which he lived, moved, and had his being; Jesus summoned the remnant to join him in this sphere.

250 A. M. Hunter. *The Work and Words of Jesus*. Philadelphia: Westminster/London: SCM, 1950. Second edition: 1973.

A good introduction for beginning students.

251 A. Finkel. *The Pharisees and the Teacher of Nazareth: A Study of Their Background, Their Halachic and Midrashic Teachings, the Similarities and Differences.* Arbeiten zur Geschichte des Spätjudentums und Urchristentums 4. Leiden: Brill, 1964.

Attempts to isolate and compare first-century Pharisaic teaching with what is regarded as Jesus' authentic teaching.

252 N. Perrin. *Rediscovering the Teaching of Jesus.* New York: Harper & Row, 1967.

An assessment of Jesus' teaching, primarily the parables, from a post-Bultmannian perspective; one of the first major studies to make comparative use of the Gospel of Thomas.

253 J. Jeremias. *New Testament Theology: The Proclamation of Jesus.* Translated by J. S. Bowden. New York: Scribner/London: SCM, 1971. Original title: *Neutestamentliche Theologie,* vol. 1: *Die Verkündigung Jesu.* Gütersloh: Mohn, 1971.

Classic statement of the Semitic background of Jesus' preaching and teaching.

254 R. H. Stein. *The Method and Message of Jesus' Teaching.* Philadelphia: Westminster, 1978.

Useful survey of the form and content of Jesus' teaching.

255 R. Hamerton-Kelly. *God the Father: Theology and Patriarchy in the Teaching of Jesus.* Overtures to Biblical Theology. Philadelphia: Fortress, 1979.

Believes that Jesus challenged patriarchal assumptions in his time.

256 G. Vermes. *The Gospel of Jesus the Jew.* Newcastle-upon-Tyne: University of Newcastle-upon-Tyne Press, 1981.

Argues that Jesus taught as a holy man that the kingdom of God was present and that God was Father.

257 F. G. Downing. "The Social Contexts of Jesus the Teacher: Construction or Reconstruction." *NTS* 33 (1987) 439–51.

Argues that Jesus' teaching would have sounded to his contemporaries like that of a Cynic teacher. See also

Downing's *Jesus and the Threat of Freedom* (London: SCM, 1987).

258 P. Perkins. *Jesus as Teacher*. Understanding Jesus Today. New York/Cambridge: Cambridge University Press, 1990.

Provides an examination of characteristics, style, and content of Jesus' teaching.

6.2 Parables of Jesus

259 A. Jülicher. *Die Gleichnisreden Jesu*. 2 vols. Freiburg: Mohr, 1888–99. Second edition: 1 vol. Tübingen: Mohr, 1910. Reprinted 1976.

Brought about major turning point in the study of the parables: parables make one basic point and are not to be allegorized; allegorical elements are inauthentic.

260 C. H. Dodd. *The Parables of the Kingdom*. London: Nisbet, 1935. Second edition: New York: Scribner, 1961.

Classic study of Jesus' parables; views parable tradition as essentially authentic.

261 W. O. E. Oesterley. *The Gospel Parables in the Light of Their Jewish Background*. New York: Macmillan/London: SPCK, 1936.

Examines some two dozen parables against their Jewish background.

262 J. Jeremias. *The Parables of Jesus*. Translated by S. H. Hooke. New Testament Library. London: SCM, 1963. Third edition: New York: Scribner, 1972. Original title: *Die Gleichnisse Jesu*. Zurich: Zwingli, 1947. Tenth edition: Göttingen: Vandenhoeck & Ruprecht, 1984.

Masterful study of the parables; much usage of Semitic language and Palestinian background. For a nontechnical summary see Jeremias's *Rediscovering the Parables* (trans. S. H. Hooke; New York: Scribner, 1966).

263 E. Linnemann. *Jesus of the Parables: Introduction and Exposition*. Translated by J. Sturdy. New York: Harper & Row, 1967. British edition: *Parables of Jesus: Introduction and Exposition*. London: SPCK, 1966. Original title: *Gleichnisse*

Jesu: Einführung und Auslegung. Göttingen: Vandenhoeck & Ruprecht, 1961. Seventh edition: 1978.

Argues that most of Jesus' parables were spoken to opponents; Jesus never allegorized.

264 J. M. Robinson. "Jesus' Parables as God Happening." Pp. 134–50 in *Jesus and the Historian: Written in Honor of Ernest Cadman Colwell.* Edited by F. T. Trotter. Philadelphia: Westminster, 1968.

Argues that the parables, in their original form (not the allegorized form often found in the Gospels), derive from Jesus.

265 J. D. Crossan. *In Parables: The Challenge of the Historical Jesus.* New York: Harper & Row, 1973.

Collection of Crossan's major studies; sees Jesus as an "oral poet" who challenged the assumptions and world view of his time; the kingdom is present and the hearers are invited to participate.

266 C. E. Carlston. *The Parables of the Triple Tradition.* Philadelphia: Fortress, 1975.

Comparative study of the parables that occur in all three Synoptic Gospels; although chiefly concerned with the layers of tradition in the Gospels, does discuss the meaning of the parables in the ministry of Jesus.

267 N. Perrin. *Jesus and the Language of the Kingdom: Symbol and Metaphor in New Testament Interpretation.* Philadelphia: Fortress/London: SCM, 1976.

Believes that the parables are extended metaphors that describe the kingdom of God, itself a symbol; optimistic that Jesus' original meaning can be recovered.

268 M. Boucher. *The Mysterious Parable: A Literary Study.* Catholic Biblical Quarterly Monograph Series 6. Washington: Catholic Biblical Association, 1977.

Contrary to A. Jülicher's emphasis (#259), Boucher believes that all of the parables convey, along with the obvious meaning, an element of mystery. See also Boucher's *Parables* (New Testament Message 7; Wilmington, Del.: Glazier, 1981).

269 W. S. Kissinger. *The Parables of Jesus: A History of Interpretation and Bibliography*. American Theological Library Association Bibliography Series 4. Metuchen, N.J.: Scarecrow/American Theological Library Association, 1979.

Valuable resource tool.

270 C. E. Carlston. "Proverbs, Maxims and the Historical Jesus." *Journal of Biblical Literature* 99 (1980) 87–105.

Argues that many of the one hundred proverbial sayings attributed to Jesus reflect Jewish wisdom traditions.

271 P. B. Payne. "Jesus' Implicit Claim to Deity in His Parables." *Trinity Journal* 2 (1981) 3–23.

Observes that in many of Jesus' parables Jesus depicts himself in language used in the Old Testament to describe God.

272 R. H. Stein. *An Introduction to the Parables of Jesus*. Philadelphia: Westminster, 1981.

Finds four themes in Jesus' parables: (1) the kingdom of God as present reality, (2) the call to decision, (3) the nature of God, and (4) final judgment.

273 B. B. Scott. "Assaying the Rock: The Authenticity of the Jesus Parable Tradition." *Forum* 2/1 (1986) 3–53.

Concludes that the burden of proof rests on those who deny the authenticity of the parable tradition; examines twenty-seven parables; bibliography.

274 D. Wenham. *The Parables of Jesus: Pictures of Revolution*. Jesus Library. London: Hodder & Stoughton, 1989.

Places parables in the context of Jesus' life and ministry, emphasizing their revolutionary character.

275 B. H. Young. *Jesus and His Jewish Parables: Rediscovering the Roots of Jesus' Teaching*. Theological Inquiries. New York: Paulist, 1989.

A valuable comparative study. A more convenient presentation will be found in #277.

276 C. Blomberg. *Interpreting the Parables*. Downers Grove, Ill./Leicester: InterVarsity, 1990.

Offers an important critique of the assumptions and methods common in parable research (such as the assumption that allegorizing parables cannot derive from Jesus); concludes that the kingdom of God is the common theme, with some parables hinting at Jesus' divinity.

277 H. K. McArthur and R. M. Johnston. *They Also Taught in Parables: Rabbinic Parables from the First Centuries of the Christian Era*. Grand Rapids: Zondervan, 1990.
Compares 125 synopticlike parables from the rabbinic materials with 28 of Jesus' parables.

6.3 Jesus' Teaching on the Kingdom of God

278 R. Schnackenburg. *God's Rule and Kingdom*. Translated by J. Murray. New York: Herder & Herder/Edinburgh/London: Nelson, 1963. Reprinted London: Search, 1968. Original title: *Gottes Herrschaft und Reich*. Freiburg: Herder, 1959.
Concludes that the kingdom of God constituted Jesus' central theme in his preaching and teaching; argues that the kingdom (*pace* C. H. Dodd) is futuristic, but it does require an immediate response.

279 N. Perrin. *The Kingdom of God in the Teaching of Jesus*. Philadelphia: Westminster/London: SCM, 1963.
Reviews history of scholarship; favors the views of some of R. Bultmann's leading pupils; interprets the futurity of the kingdom in existential terms.

280 G. E. Ladd. *Jesus and the Kingdom*. New York: Harper & Row, 1964/London: SPCK, 1966.
Argues that according to Jesus' proclamation the kingdom of God is both realized and yet will come in its fullness in the eschaton.

281 B. D. Chilton. *God in Strength: Jesus' Announcement of the Kingdom*. Studien zum Neuen Testament und seiner Umwelt B/1. Freistadt: Plöchl, 1979. Reprinted Sheffield: JSOT Press, 1987.
Argues that Jesus' announcement of the kingdom should be understood to mean that God was present "in strength" among people.

282 T. F. Glasson. *Jesus and the End of the World*. Edinburgh: St. Andrews, 1980.

Argues that in calling and training disciples Jesus clearly did not believe that the world was about to end.

283 O. Betz. "Jesus' Gospel of the Kingdom." Pp. 53–74 in *The Gospel and the Gospels*. Edited by P. Stuhlmacher. Translated by J. S. Bowden. Grand Rapids: Eerdmans, 1991. Original title: "Jesu Evangelium vom Gottesreich." Pp. 55–77 in *Das Evangelium und die Evangelien: Vorträge vom Tübinger Symposium 1982*. Edited by P. Stuhlmacher. WUNT 28. Tübingen: Mohr, 1983.

Concludes that Jesus borrowed the word *gospel* and its concept from Isaiah 52–53, thus implying that he saw himself as the Suffering Servant.

284 G. W. Buchanan. *Jesus: The King and His Kingdom*. Macon, Ga.: Mercer University Press, 1984.

In some ways eccentric, argues that Jesus attempted to establish a kingdom through military means.

285 B. D. Chilton (ed.). *The Kingdom of God in the Teaching of Jesus*. Issues in Religion and Theology 5. Philadelphia: Fortress/London: SPCK, 1984.

Articles by R. Otto, W. G. Kümmel, N. Perrin (excerpts from #267), B. D. Chilton (excerpts from #281), and others.

286 G. R. Beasley-Murray. *Jesus and the Kingdom of God*. Grand Rapids: Eerdmans, 1986.

Concludes that in Jesus' appearance and proclamation the kingdom of God has begun to operate on earth; with Jesus' arrival the kingdom is present, not merely foreshadowed, but it is not, however, realized fully, for the fullness of the kingdom will arrive some day in the future; the kingdom has begun, but it is yet to be consummated.

287 M. J. Borg. "A Temperate Case for a Non-Eschatological Jesus." *Forum* 2/3 (1986) 81–102.

Argues that when the Son of Man sayings are denied authenticity, there are no exegetical grounds for understanding Jesus' proclamation of the kingdom as eschatological; concludes that Jesus' message came to be understood as eschatological by the early church because of Jesus' resurrection, an event associated with the eschaton.

288 G. R. Beasley-Murray. "Jesus and the Kingdom of God." *Baptist Quarterly* 32 (1987) 141–46.

When Jesus spoke of the "kingdom of God" he was speaking of salvation.

289 M. D. Hooker. "Traditions about the Temple in the Sayings of Jesus." *Bulletin of the John Rylands University Library of Manchester* 70 (1988) 7–19.

Contrary to E. P. Sanders (#132), claims that Jesus may have intended to cleanse the temple.

290 M. N. A. Bockmuehl. "Why Did Jesus Predict the Destruction of the Temple?" *Crux* 25/3 (1989) 11–18.

Concludes that Jesus predicted the destruction of the temple as an objection against corruption and as an announcement of coming judgment and restoration.

291 C. A. Evans. "Jesus' Action in the Temple: Cleansing or Portent of Destruction?" *CBQ* 51 (1989) 237–70.

Argues that Jesus' action in the temple, *pace* E. P. Sanders (#132), was a messianic purge directed against temple polity.

6.4 Sermon on the Mount and the Ethics of Jesus

292 G. Friedlander. *The Jewish Sources of the Sermon on the Mount.* New York: Bloch, 1911. Reprinted New York: Ktav, 1969.

Citing what are regarded as relevant parallels, suggests how Jesus' original sermon and teachings have been Christianized.

293 H. Windisch. *The Meaning of the Sermon on the Mount.* Translated by S. M. Gilmour. Philadelphia: Westminster, 1951. Original title: *Der Sinn der Bergpredigt.* Leipzig: Hinrichs, 1929. Second edition: 1937.

Argues that Jesus, much as an orthodox Jew, required a higher ethic of obedience to the law and perhaps saw himself as an authoritative interpreter of the law, but not as the Messiah.

294 J. Jeremias. *The Sermon on the Mount.* Translated by N. Perrin. Philadelphia: Fortress, 1963/London: Athlone, 1961.

Original title: *Die Bergpredigt*. Calwer Hefte 27. Stuttgart:
Calwer, 1959. Second edition: 1960.

Attempts to discover the original setting of the Sermon on
the Mount in Jesus' life; concludes that the sermon is
made up of smaller units, themselves often summaries of
larger sermons. Underlying these units ("apodoses") is the
protasis of Jesus' message ("your sins are forgiven").
Because their sins are forgiven, Jesus can make the ethical
demands found in the Sermon on the Mount.

295 J. A. Baird. *The Justice of God in the Teachings of Jesus*. Philadelphia: Westminster/London: SCM, 1963.

Believes that the idea of the justice of God is central to
Jesus' teachings, an idea that stands in continuity with
Israel's prophetic tradition.

296 W. D. Davies. *The Setting of the Sermon on the Mount*. Cambridge: Cambridge University Press, 1964.

Argues that although the Sermon on the Mount is itself a
literary creation, its contents largely represent the authentic teachings of Jesus; concludes that Jesus not only
preached eschatology, but also made ethical demands,
making known the true law, namely, that it is God himself who is the "law."

297 V. P. Furnish. *The Love Command in the New Testament*.
Nashville: Abingdon, 1972.

Concludes that "Jesus' commandment to *love* the enemy
[is what] most of all sets his ethic of love apart from other
'love ethics' of antiquity" (p. 66). This teaching arises in
part out of Jesus' proclamation that the kingdom of God is
coming.

298 W. S. Kissinger. *The Sermon on the Mount: A History of
Interpretation and Bibliography*. American Theological Li-
brary Association Bibliography Series 3. Metuchen, N.J.:
Scarecrow/American Theological Library Association, 1975.

Helpful survey and bibliography.

299 J. Piper. *"Love Your Enemies": Jesus' Love Command in the
Synoptic Gospels and in the Early Christian Paraenesis; A
History of the Tradition and Interpretation of Its Use*.

SNTSMS 38. Cambridge: Cambridge University Press, 1979. Reprinted Grand Rapids: Baker, 1991.

Argues that Jesus commanded love of enemies in light of the presence of the kingdom of God.

300 R. A. Guelich. *The Sermon on the Mount: A Foundation for Understanding*. Waco, Tex.: Word, 1982.

Concludes that, although the Sermon on the Mount is a literary creation of the Matthean evangelist, it is made up of traditional materials which go back to Jesus himself.

301 G. Strecker. *The Sermon on the Mount: An Exegetical Commentary*. Translated by O. C. Dean Jr. Nashville: Abingdon/ Edinburgh: T. & T. Clark, 1988. Original title: *Die Bergpredigt: Ein exegetischer Kommentar*. Göttingen: Vandenhoeck & Ruprecht, 1984.

A detailed exegesis of the Sermon on the Mount; concludes that, although serving the theological interests of the Matthean evangelist, the core of the sermon may be traced back to the preaching of Jesus.

302 C. Bauman. *The Sermon on the Mount: A Modern Quest for Its Meaning*. Macon, Ga.: Mercer University Press, 1985.

Survey of the major studies on the Sermon on the Mount; bibliography.

303 H. D. Betz. *Essays on the Sermon on the Mount*. Translated by L. Welborn. Philadelphia: Fortress, 1985. Original title: *Studien zur Bergpredigt*. Tübingen: Mohr, 1985.

Views the Sermon on the Mount as an early pre-Matthean epitome of Jesus' teaching. A forthcoming technical commentary in the Hermeneia series will present exegetical details.

304 W. Wink. "Neither Passivity nor Violence: Jesus' Third Way." *SBLSP* 27 (1988) 210–24.

Studying Matt 5:38–42, argues that Jesus taught that evil should be actively resisted, but not through violence.

305 B. Wiebe. "Messianic Ethics: Response to the Kingdom of God." *Interp* 45 (1991) 29–42.

Concludes that Jesus did not negate the law, but in some ways his teaching transcended it.

6.5 Jesus and Prayer

306 J. Jeremias. *The Prayers of Jesus.* Translated by J. S. Bowden.
SBT 6. Naperville, Ill.: Allenson/London: SCM, 1967.

A selection of studies from Jeremias's *Das Vater-Unser im
Lichte der neueren Forschung* (Calwer Hefte 50; Stuttgart:
Calwer, 1962; third edition: 1965) (previously translated as
The Lord's Prayer [Facet Books, Biblical Series 8; Philadel-
phia: Fortress, 1964]) and *Abba: Studien zur neutesta-
mentlichen Theologie und Zeitgeschichte* (Göttingen:
Vandenhoeck & Ruprecht, 1966), pp. 15–80 and 145–52
(pp. 152–71 from *Das Vater-Unser*). Especially helpful for
Semitic background.

307 R. S. Barbour. "Gethsemane in the Tradition of the Passion."
NTS 16 (1969–70) 231–51.

Argues that the tradition that Jesus prayed before his passion is strongly attested and should be regarded as authentic.

308 C. A. Blaising. "Gethsemane: A Prayer of Faith." *JETS* 22
(1979) 333–43.

Accepting the authenticity of Jesus' Gethsemane prayer,
concludes that Jesus prayed not to avoid the crisis, but
that it might pass quickly.

309 R. Hamerton-Kelly. "God the Father in the Bible and in the
Experience of Jesus." Pp. 95–162 in *God as Father?* Edited by
J. Metz and E. Schillebeeckx. Concilium 143. New York:
Seabury, 1981.

Argues that Jesus' understanding of God as Father was one
of the most important aspects of Jesus' self-understanding,
an aspect that lay at the heart of his teaching and ministry.

310 D. Zeller. "God as Father in the Proclamation and in the
Prayer of Jesus." Translated by N. Quigley, A. Finkel, and L.
Frizzell. Pp. 117–29 in *Standing before God: Studies on
Prayer in Scripture and in Tradition with Essays in Honor of
John M. Oesterreicher.* Edited by A. Finkel and L. Frizzell.
New York: Ktav, 1981.

Notes that God as Father in Jesus' authentic prayers and
teaching tends to appear in wisdom sayings; concludes

that Israel is being admonished to restore its filial relationship with God.

311 M. Dorneich (ed.). *Vater-Unser Bibliographie—The Lord's Prayer: A Bibliography*. Freiburg: Herder, 1982.

A 141-page bibliography of books and articles.

6.6 Jesus and the Law (and Old Testament)

312 B. H. Branscomb. *Jesus and the Law of Moses*. New York: Smith, 1930.

Argues that Jesus elevated the ethical aspects of the law and relegated the ritual aspects to a secondary position.

313 T. W. Manson. "The Old Testament in the Teaching of Jesus." *Bulletin of the John Rylands University Library of Manchester* 34 (1951–52) 312–32.

Classic essay; examines the portions of the Old Testament that Jesus quoted, the form of the text cited (Hebrew and targumic traces are present), and his principles of interpretation.

314 R. T. France. *Jesus and the Old Testament*. London: Tyndale, 1971.

Argues that Jesus understood himself in the light of various Old Testament personalities (David, Solomon, Elijah, Jonah, Isaiah), institutions (priesthood, covenant), and prophecies (humiliation, service).

315 K. Berger. *Die Gesetzesauslegung Jesu: Ihr historischer Hintergrund im Judentum und im Alten Testament*. Wissenschaftliche Monographien zum Alten und Neuen Testament 40. Neukirchen-Vluyn: Neukirchener Verlag, 1972.

A massive study, particularly valuable for background material. Most of the discussion on Jesus' understanding of the law centers on Mark 7:6–13; 10:19; 12:28–34; Matt 19:16–22; Luke 18:18–23.

316 R. N. Longenecker. *Biblical Exegesis in the Apostolic Period*. Grand Rapids: Eerdmans, 1974. Reprinted 1977.

On pp. 51–78 surveys the appearance and function of the Old Testament in Jesus' teaching.

317 R. J. Banks. *Jesus and the Law in the Synoptic Tradition.*
SNTSMS 28. Cambridge: Cambridge University Press, 1975.

Argues that Jesus' attitude toward the law has been accurately preserved in the synoptic tradition; concludes that
Jesus does not oppose the law, but neither does he try to
justify his teachings by appeal to the law.

318 S. Westerholm. *Jesus and Scribal Authority.* Lund: Gleerup,
1978.

Compares Jesus against the teachers of the law of his time;
concludes that Jesus taught that God's will sometimes
transcends God's law.

319 J. A. T. Robinson. "Did Jesus Have a Distinctive Use of Scripture?" Pp. 49–57 and 266 in *Christological Perspectives: Essays in Honor of Harvey K. McArthur.* Edited by R. F. Berkey
and S. A. Edwards. New York: Pilgrim, 1982. Reprinted in
Robinson's *Twelve More New Testament Studies*, pp. 35–43.
London: SCM, 1984.

Argues that Jesus' "challenging use" of Scripture is distinctive to Jesus (e.g., Mark 2:25; 9:12; 12:10, 26) and so
probably points to authentic tradition.

320 B. D. Chilton. *A Galilean Rabbi and His Bible: Jesus' Use of
the Interpreted Scripture of His Time.* Good News Studies 8.
Wilmington, Del.: Glazier, 1984. British edition: *A Galilean
Rabbi and His Bible: Jesus' Own Interpretation of Isaiah.*
London: SPCK, 1984.

A study of the dictional and thematic coherence of Jesus'
teaching with early traditions in the Isaiah Targum.

321 D. J. Moo. "Jesus and the Authority of the Mosaic Law."
JSNT 20 (1984) 3–49.

Argues that Jesus obeyed the law, but also understood it as
fulfilled because of his advent.

322 E. P. Sanders. *Jesus and Judaism.* Philadelphia: Fortress/Lon-
don: SCM, 1985.

See esp. pp. 245–69. Argues that Jesus accepted the law
and offered no criticism of it. See also annotation at #132.

323 R. P. Booth. *Jesus and the Laws of Purity: Tradition History and Legal History in Mark 7.* Journal for the Study of the New Testament Supplement 13. Sheffield: JSOT Press, 1986.
Argues that Jesus' emphasis of moral purity over cultic purity gave rise to subsequent controversy in the early church.

324 P. Sigal. *The Halakah of Jesus of Nazareth according to the Gospel of Matthew.* Lanham, Md.: University Press of America, 1986.
Argues that Jesus' halakah was essentially in agreement with the pre-Jamnian rabbis.

325 H. Weiss. "The Sabbath in the Synoptic Gospels." *JSNT* 38 (1990) 13–27.
Concludes that Jesus did not challenge the Sabbath law.

7

Jesus' Self-Understanding

Research in the life of Jesus often raises the question of how
Jesus understood himself. Did he think of himself as the Messiah, and if he did, in what sense? Did Jesus call himself the Son
of Man, and if he did, what did he mean by this self-designation?
Other questions have to do with his intentions. What did he
expect to accomplish in Jerusalem? Did he foresee his death? All
of these questions are fundamental for life-of-Jesus research. The
bibliography represents scholarship addressed to these questions.

326 J. Jeremias. *The Eucharistic Words of Jesus.* Translated by N.
Perrin. Oxford: Oxford University Press, 1955. Revised edition: New York/London: Scribner, 1966. Original title: *Die
Abendmahlsworte Jesu.* Göttingen: Vandenhoeck & Ruprecht, 1935. Third edition: 1960.
Discusses the nature of the Last Supper, when it took
place, and what it meant to Jesus and his disciples; concludes that Jesus anticipated his death and understood it
to have redemptive significance.

327 E. Stauffer. "Messias oder Menschensohn." *NovT* 1 (1956)
81–102.
Argues that Jesus called himself "Son of Man" and not
"Messiah" to avoid association with popular resistance
movements.

328 H. E. Tödt. *The Son of Man in the Synoptic Tradition.* Translated by D. M. Barton. Philadelphia: Westminster/London:
SCM, 1965. Original title: *Der Menschensohn in der synop-*

tischen Überlieferung. Gütersloh: Mohn, 1959. Second edition: 1963.

Judgmental Son of Man sayings are viewed as authentic, but sayings about serving and suffering are not.

329 P. W. Meyer. "The Problem of the Messianic Self-Consciousness of Jesus." *NovT* 4 (1960) 122–38.

Reviews the works of the major contributors to the debate, for example, H. S. Reimarus, A. Schweitzer, W. Wrede, E. Schweizer, and H. E. Tödt.

330 F. Hahn. *The Titles of Jesus in Christology: Their History in Early Christianity.* Translated by H. Knight and G. Ogg. New York: World/London: Lutterworth, 1969. Original title: *Christologische Hoheitstitel: Ihre Geschichte im frühen Christentum.* Forschungen zur Religion und Literatur des Alten und Neuen Testaments 83. Göttingen: Vandenhoeck & Ruprecht, 1962. Second edition: 1964.

Argues that Jesus called himself the "Son of Man," but only in reference to the apocalyptic Son of Man. Jesus was born in the line of David and so was called the "son of David."

331 O. Betz. "Die Frage nach dem messianischen Bewusstsein Jesu." *NovT* 6 (1963) 20–48.

Argues against R. Bultmann, E. Käsemann, and G. Bornkamm, who had argued that Jesus never claimed to be Messiah. Jesus' threat to rebuild the temple provides the best evidence that Jesus did in fact understand himself as Israel's Messiah.

332 P. Vielhauer. "Jesus und der Menschensohn: Zur Diskussion mit Heinz Eduard Tödt und Eduard Schweizer." *ZTK* 60 (1963) 133–77.

Views the Son of Man sayings as inauthentic; they were employed by the evangelists to demonstrate the authority of the earthly Jesus.

333 I. H. Marshall. "The Synoptic Son of Man Sayings in Recent Discussion." *NTS* 12 (1965–66) 327–51.

Criticizes those who have denied the authenticity of some or all of the Son of Man sayings; concludes that Jesus chose this self-designation to hide his messianic identity from his opponents.

334 N. Perrin. "The Son of Man in Ancient Judaism and Primitive Christianity: A Suggestion." *Biblical Research* 11 (1966) 17–28.

Argues that there was no apocalyptic "Son of Man" concept in early Judaism; hence there could not have been such a concept in the teaching of Jesus or in his self-understanding.

335 F. H. Borsch. *The Son of Man in Myth and History.* New Testament Library. Philadelphia: Westminster/London: SCM, 1967.

Compares New Testament Son of Man sayings with a variety of related concepts in antiquity.

336 R. E. Brown. "How Much Did Jesus Know?—A Survey of the Biblical Evidence." *CBQ* 29 (1967) 315–45.

Argues that Jesus anticipated his rejection, death, and vindication and thought of himself as God's agent (not necessarily Messiah) for establishing the kingdom.

337 R. E. Brown. *Jesus, God and Man: Modern Biblical Reflections.* Milwaukee: Bruce, 1967.

Concerned with the question of deity and self-understanding of the historical Jesus.

338 I. H. Marshall. "The Divine Sonship of Jesus." *Interp* 21 (1967) 87–103.

Concludes that Jesus understood himself as the unique Son of God.

339 R. T. France. "The Servant of the Lord in the Teaching of Jesus." *Tyndale Bulletin* 19 (1968) 26–52.

Argues that Jesus understood himself as the Servant of Isaiah 53, as well as the Son of Man of Daniel 7.

340 J. C. O'Neill. "The Silence of Jesus." *NTS* 15 (1968–69) 153–67.

Argues that Jesus did not refer to himself as "Messiah" because to do so was blasphemous; God would recognize one as the true Messiah at enthronement. Jesus' silence is therefore itself part of implicit Christology.

341 R. N. Longenecker. "'Son of Man' as a Self-Designation of Jesus." *JETS* 12 (1969) 151–58.

Concludes that, alluding to Daniel 7, Jesus called himself the Son of Man, an expression connoting suffering and glory.

342 W. Klassen. "Jesus and the Zealot Option." *Canadian Journal of Theology* 16 (1970) 12–21.

Argues that although Jesus was attracted to the zealots' high regard for the law, he eschewed their tendency toward violence.

343 I. H. Marshall. "The Son of Man in Contemporary Debate." *Evangelical Quarterly* 42 (1970) 67–87.

Concludes that the Son of Man tradition in the New Testament goes back to Jesus himself.

344 D. E. Aune. "A Note on Jesus' Messianic Consciousness and 11QMelchizedek." *Evangelical Quarterly* 45 (1973) 161–65.

Argues that the interpretation of Isa 52:7 in 11QMelch 15–19 is evidence that preaching good news was understood as part of the messianic task. Since Jesus preached good news, he may very well have thought of himself as the Messiah.

345 R. Pesch and R. Schnackenburg (eds.). *Jesus und der Menschensohn: Für Anton Vögtle.* Freiburg: Herder, 1975.

Twenty-five studies on the expression "Son of Man"; of particular relevance to the question of the historical Jesus are those by A. J. B. Higgins, H. Schürmann, R. Pesch, J. Gnilka, W. G. Kümmel, K. Kertelge, and F. Hahn.

346 R. Bauckham. "The Sonship of the Historical Jesus in Christology." *SJT* 31 (1978) 245–60.

Argues that Jesus' sense of mission derives from his sense of being God's Son.

347 G. Beckerlegge. "Jesus' Authority and the Problem of His Self-Consciousness." *Heythrop Journal* 19 (1978) 365–82.

Reviews the obstacles that make it difficult to determine Jesus' self-understanding; *pace* R. Bultmann, maintains that apart from such knowledge one cannot assign meaning to Jesus' death.

348 A. J. B. Higgins. *The Son of Man in the Teaching of Jesus.* SNTSMS 39. Cambridge: Cambridge University Press, 1980.

Argues that Jesus expected vindication after his death in the form of his installation as Son of Man who will come in judgment.

349 R. G. Gruenler. "Implied Christological Claims in the Core
Sayings of Jesus: An Application of Wittgenstein's Phenomenology." *SBLSP* 20 (1981) 65–77.

Applying L. Wittgenstein's phenomenology of persons to
Jesus' core sayings (as defined by N. Perrin in #252), concludes that a new approach to investigating Jesus' self-
understanding is opened up.

350 P. Stuhlmacher. "Vicariously Giving His Life for Many:
Mark 10:45 (Matt. 20:38)." Pp. 16–29 in Stuhlmacher's *Rec-
onciliation, Law, and Righteousness: Essays in Biblical
Theology.* Translated by E. R. Kalin. Philadelphia: Fortress,
1986. Original title: "Existenzstellvertretung für die Vielen:
Mk 10,45 (Mt 20,28)." Pp. 27–42 in Stuhlmacher's *Versöhn-
ung, Gesetz und Gerechtigkeit: Aufsätze zur biblischen Theologie.* Göttingen: Vandenhoeck & Ruprecht, 1981.

Argues that Jesus reversed the idea found in Daniel that
the Son of Man was to be served. See the similar study by
W. Grimm (#356).

351 B. D. Chilton. "Jesus *ben David*: Reflections on the
Davidssohnfrage." *JSNT* 14 (1982) 88–112.

Discusses in what sense Jesus viewed himself as the son
of David; concludes that Jesus saw himself as son of David
(Mark 12:35), but not in sense of scribal messianic expectation.

352 R. Leivestad. *Jesus in His Own Perspective: An Examination
of His Sayings, Actions, and Eschatological Titles.* Translated by D. E. Aune. Minneapolis: Augsburg, 1987. Original
title: *Hvem ville Jesus vaere?* Oslo: Land og Kirke–Gyldendal
Norsk, 1982.

Argues that at his baptism Jesus perceived his call to be
Messiah, to which his subsequent teaching and actions
gave witness.

353 S. Kim. *The "Son of Man" as the Son of God.* WUNT 30.
Tübingen: Mohr, 1983.

Argues that the Son of Man sayings represent Jesus'
attempt to identify himself as Son of God as inoffensively
as possible.

354 B. Lindars. *Jesus, Son of Man: A Fresh Examination of the Son of Man Sayings in the Gospels in the Light of Recent Research.* Grand Rapids: Eerdmans, 1984/London: SPCK, 1983.

Argues that Jesus' use of "Son of Man" had nothing to do with an apocalyptic figure, but only meant "one like me."

355 L. Sabourin. "About Jesus' Self-Understanding." *Religious Studies Bulletin* 3 (1983) 129–34.

Argues that Jesus understood himself as the Servant of God, fulfilling the prophecy of Daniel 7.

356 W. Grimm. *Jesus und das Danielbuch,* vol. 1: *Jesu Einspruch gegen das Offenbarungsystem Daniels (Mt 11,25–27; Lk 17,20–21).* Arbeiten zum Neuen Testament und Judentum 6/1. New York/Frankfurt am Main: Lang, 1984.

Concludes that Jesus opposed the esoteric stance seen in the Book of Daniel by claiming that the mysteries of the kingdom have been withheld "from the wise and learned, and revealed to babes" (Matt 11:25). See also the second volume by O. Betz (#358). A similar conclusion was reached by P. Stuhlmacher (#350).

357 W. G. Kümmel. *Jesus der Menschensohn?* Stuttgart: Steiner, 1984.

Provides an excellent bibliography (pp. 41–46) and survey of research on the problem of the Son of Man sayings since H. J. Holtzmann.

358 O. Betz. *Jesus und das Danielbuch,* vol. 2: *Die Menschensohnworte Jesu und die Zukunftserwartung des Paulus (Daniel 7,13–14).* Arbeiten zum Neuen Testament und Judentum 6/2. New York/Frankfurt am Main: Lang, 1985.

Argues that Jesus reinterpreted ideas in Daniel to teach his contemporaries that the Son of Man was to serve, not be served. See also the first volume (#356).

359 H. F. Bayer. *Jesus' Predictions of Vindication and Resurrection: The Provenance, Meaning and Correlation of the Synoptic Predictions.* WUNT 2/20. Tübingen: Mohr, 1986.

Concludes that Jesus did predict his suffering and vindication.

360 M. de Jonge. "Jesus, Son of David and Son of God." Pp. 95–
104 in *Intertextuality in Biblical Writings: Essays in Honour
of Bas van Iersel.* Edited by S. Draisma. Kampen: Kol, 1989.
Believes that Jesus called himself "Son of Man" (an
expression to which Jesus gave a distinctive meaning) and
by addressing God as his Father implied a unique relationship to the Deity, from which his earliest followers
deduced his divine sonship.

361 C. A. Evans. "Jesus' Action in the Temple: Cleansing or Portent of Destruction?" *CBQ* 51 (1989) 237–70.
Contrary to E. P. Sanders (#132), argues that Jesus did not
threaten to destroy the temple, but, criticizing corruption
and polity of ruling priests, prophesied its destruction.

362 C. A. Evans. "Jesus' Action in the Temple and Evidence of
Corruption in the First-Century Temple." *SBLSP* 28 (1989)
522–39.
Assesses the widespread evidence of corruption in the
temple establishment of Jesus' day, arguing that Jesus'
self-understanding must in part be understood against this
background.

363 B. Witherington III. *The Christology of Jesus.* Minneapolis:
Fortress, 1990.
Based on an assessment of the christological implications
to be inferred from Jesus' relationships, deeds, and words,
Witherington concludes that Jesus understood himself as
God's agent of salvation.

364 D. J. Antwi. "Did Jesus Consider His Death to Be an Atoning
Sacrifice?" *Interp* 45 (1991) 17–28.
Argues that Jesus acted in various ways (such as forgiving
sins and speaking and acting against the temple) that suggest that he did regard his death as an atoning sacrifice.

365 C. A. Evans. "In What Sense 'Blasphemy'? Jesus before Caiaphas in Mark 14:61–64." *SBLSP* 30 (1991) 215–34.
Argues that Jesus' reply to Caiaphas is authentic and
coheres with other dominical tradition based on the imag-
ery of Daniel 7 (e.g., Mark 10:37–40; Matt 19:28 ‖ Luke
22:28–30).

8

Miracles of Jesus

At one time viewed as later inauthentic embellishments and so disregarded, the miracle tradition is now viewed as having a historical basis irrespective of how the phenomena are to be explained. Current studies focus on the social dimension of miracles in the life of Jesus and, primarily, in the life of the early church.

366 R. Bultmann. "The Problem of Miracle." Translated by F. D. Gealy. *Religion in Life* 27 (1958) 63–75. Original title: "Zur Frage des Wunders." Pp. 214–28 in Bultmann's *Glauben und Verstehen*, vol. 1. Tübingen: Mohr, 1954.

> Argues that the idea of miracle, as an event contrary to nature, "can no longer be maintained. Miracle is an act of God in distinction from a natural event. Faith in God and in miracle mean exactly the same thing" (p. 69). The only miracle is that of revelation whereby the hidden God makes himself known. The question of facticity of Jesus' miracles is irrelevant. The miracle stories testify to the nature of Christian faith; to respond in faith to God is to believe in God in whatever manner he may chose to reveal himself.

367 H. van der Loos, *The Miracles of Jesus*. Novum Testamentum Supplement 9. Leiden: Brill, 1965.

A massive study that defines "miracle" and reviews Jesus' miracles in the context of his time; concludes that the gospel accounts are historically reliable.

368 C. F. D. Moule (ed.). *Miracles: Cambridge Studies in Their Philosophy and History.* London: Mowbray, 1965.

Twelve studies on miracles in the Old Testament, New Testament, and ancient world; most relevant for historical-Jesus research are those by B. Lindars, "Elijah, Elisha and the Gospel Miracles" (pp. 61–79), and M. E. Glasswell, "The Use of Miracles in the Markan Gospel" (pp. 149–62).

369 A. Vögtle. "The Miracles of Jesus against Their Contemporary Background." Pp. 96–105 in *Jesus in His Time.* Edited by H. J. Schultz. Translated by B. Watchorn. Philadelphia: Fortress/London: SPCK, 1971. Original title: "Jesu Wundertaten vor dem Hintergrund ihrer Zeit." Pp. 83–90 in *Die Zeit Jesu.* Edited by H. J. Schultz. Stuttgart: Kreuz, 1966.

Compares Jesus' miracles to miracle traditions outside the New Testament; concludes that Jesus' miracles are unique in many respects.

370 F. Mussner. *The Miracles of Jesus: An Introduction.* Translated by A. Wimmer. Notre Dame, Ind.: University of Notre Dame Press, 1968. Original title: *Die Wunder Jesu: Eine Hinführung.* Schriften zur Katechetik 10. Munich: Kösel, 1967.

Argues that the miracles of Jesus in the Gospels portray the *ipsissima facta Jesu.*

371 A. Suhl. *Die Wunder Jesu: Ereignis und Überlieferung.* Gütersloh: Mohn, 1968.

Argues that the miracle tradition ultimately is rooted in the historical Jesus, not the life of the early community.

372 R. Pesch. *Jesu ureigene Taten? Ein Beitrag zur Wunderfrage.* Quaestiones Disputatae 52. Freiburg: Herder, 1970.

Explores the possibility of establishing the *ipsissima facta Jesu,* as F. Mussner argued (#370); concludes that if the *ipsissima verba Jesu* cannot be established, neither can the *ipsissima facta* be established.

373 C. E. Carlston. "The Question of Miracles." *Andover Newton Quarterly* 12 (1971) 99–107.

Argues that the miracles of Jesus were manifestations of God, but apart from Christian faith they are subject to diverse and opposing interpretations.

374 R. Latourelle. "Authenticité historique des miracles de Jésus: Essai de critériologie." *Gregorianum* 54 (1973) 225–62. (English translation of pp. 229–61 in #385, pp. 54–69.)

Discusses criteria for assessing the historicity of the miracles of Jesus; believes that evidence and logic support their historicity.

375 G. Theissen. *The Miracle Stories of Early Christian Tradition*. Translated by F. McDonagh. Edited by J. K. Riches. Philadelphia: Fortress/Edinburgh: T. & T. Clark, 1983. Original title: *Urchristliche Wundergeschichten: Ein Beitrag zur form-geschichtlichen Erforschung der synoptischen Evangelien*. Studien zum Neuen Testament 8. Gütersloh: Mohn, 1974.

A form- and social-critical analysis of early Christian miracle tradition; for Jesus' miracles see especially pp. 277–80.

376 P. J. Achtemeier. "Miracles and the Historical Jesus: A Study of Mark 9:14–29." *CBQ* 37 (1975) 471–91.

Argues that the miracle tradition underlying Mark 9:14–29 probably reflects something that Jesus actually did.

377 X. Léon-Dufour (ed.). *Les miracles de Jésus: Selon le Nouveau Testament*. Paris: Seuil, 1977.

Essays by several scholars comparing the miracles of Jesus with ancient miracle traditions.

378 L. Sabourin. *The Divine Miracles Discussed and Defended*. Rome: Catholic Books, 1977.

A reprint of essays that appeared in *Biblical Theology Bulletin* 1 (1971) 59–80; 4 (1974) 115–75; 5 (1975) 146–200, plus new chapters on miracles in the early and modern church; concludes that the gospel miracle stories are essentially historical.

379 H. C. Kee. *Miracle in the Early Christian World: A Study in Socio-historical Method* (esp. pp. 146–73). New Haven/London: Yale University Press, 1983.

Discusses the history of the miracle tradition and how Jesus' miracles may have been interpreted in the first-century context.

380 C. L. Blomberg. "New Testament Miracles and Higher Criticism: Climbing up the Slippery Slope." *JETS* 27 (1984) 425–38.
     Observes an emerging consensus among scholars to view the miracles as having metaphorical significance, but not necessarily as being unhistorical.

381 C. Brown. *Miracles and the Critical Mind*. Grand Rapids: Eerdmans/Exeter: Paternoster, 1984.
     A review of the evolution of critical thinking with regard to miracles; concludes that the miracles of Jesus enjoy historical support and probably should be viewed as factual.

382 D. Smith. "Jesus and the Pharisees in Socio-Anthropological Perspective." *Trinity Journal* 6 (1985) 151–56.
     Examines Jesus' healing activities against a Pharisaic background.

383 C. Brown. "Synoptic Miracle Stories: A Jewish Religious and Social Setting." *Forum* 2/4 (1986) 55–76.
     Argues that Jesus' critics saw his miracles as the signs of a false prophet (cf. Mark 8:1–13; Deut 13:1–5).

384 D. J. Graham. "Jesus as Miracle Worker." *Scottish Bulletin of Evangelical Theology* 4 (1986) 85–96.
     Evaluates recent discussion, especially that of G. Vermes, A. E. Harvey, and E. P. Sanders.

385 R. Latourelle. *The Miracles of Jesus and the Theology of Miracles*. Translated by M. J. O'Connell. New York: Paulist, 1988. Original title: *Miracles de Jésus et théologie du miracle*. Recherches n.s. 8. Paris: Cerf/Montreal: Bellarmin, 1986.
     Examines historicity of Jesus' sayings regarding his miracles.

386 D. Wenham and C. L. Blomberg (eds.). *The Miracles of Jesus*. Gospel Perspectives 6. Sheffield: JSOT Press, 1986.
     Very important volume, consisting of twelve studies that assess the historical problem of Jesus' miracles and their interpretation in modern scholarship. See especially W. L. Craig, "The Problem of Miracles: A Historical and Philo-

sophical Perspective" (pp. 9–48); G. Maier, "Zur neutestamentlichen Wunderexegese im 19. und 20. Jahrhundert" (pp. 49–87; "historische Forschung kann heute mit guten Gründen sagen, dass Jesus damals Wunder getan hat" [p. 79]); B. D. Chilton, "Exorcism and History: Mark 1:21–28" (pp. 253–71; "the historical question centers fundamentally on what people perceived, and how they acted on their perception" [p. 265]); and G. H. Twelftree, "εἰ δὲ ... ἐγὼ ἐκβάλλω τὰ δαιμόνια ..." (pp. 361–400; "[there is] more than sufficient evidence to affirm that Jesus was an extremely successful exorcist" [p. 393]).

387 J. Engelbrecht. "Trends in Miracle Research." *Neotestamentica* 22 (1988) 139–61.

Examines current trends and makes suggestions for future study.

9

Death of Jesus

A major issue in historical-Jesus research is understanding the factors that led to Jesus' trial and crucifixion. The grounds for his execution should help in understanding something about his ministry and the influence it had on the people of first-century Palestine.

388 H. Danby. "The Bearing of the Rabbinical Criminal Code on the Jewish Trial Narratives in the Gospels." *Journal of Theological Studies* 21 (1920) 51–76.

Concludes that "the Jewish authorities in Jerusalem were empowered to carry out no more than a preliminary investigation of the evidence against their prisoner, and a study of the gospel narratives makes it doubtful whether they can justly be said to have overstepped this permission" (pp. 75–76).

389 S. Zeitlin. *Who Crucified Jesus?* New York: Harper, 1942.

Argues that responsibility for Jesus' death lay primarily with the Romans. See also Zeitlin's studies in *Jewish Quarterly Review* 31 (1940–41) 327–69; 32 (1941–42) 175–89, 279–301; 53 (1962–63) 77–88; 55 (1964–65) 8–22.

390 J. Blinzler. *The Trial of Jesus.* Translated by I. McHugh and F. McHugh. Westminster, Md.: Newman, 1959. Original title: *Der Prozess Jesu: Das jüdische und das römische Gerichtsverfahren gegen Jesus Christus auf Grund der ältesten Zeug-*

nisse dargestellt und beurteilt. Bibelwissenschaftliche Reihe 4. Stuttgart: Katholisches Bibelwerk, 1951. Fourth edition: Regensburg: Pustet, 1969.

> Concludes that there were two trials, one Jewish and one Roman, and both called for the death sentence; chief responsibility lay with Jewish authorities. See fourth edition for bibliography (pp. 453–64).

391 G. D. Kilpatrick. *The Trial of Jesus.* London: Oxford University Press, 1953.

> Accepting the Marcan narrative as essentially reliable, concludes that the Sanhedrin interrogated Jesus, condemned him, and handed him over to Pilate for further interrogation.

392 M. Black. "The Arrest and Trial of Jesus and the Date of the Last Supper." Pp. 19–33 in *New Testament Essays: Studies in Memory of Thomas Walter Manson.* Edited by A. J. B. Higgins. Manchester: Manchester University Press, 1959.

> Argues that "the period occupied by the arrest and trial of Jesus was longer than our Gospels make it out to be" (p. 32).

393 P. Winter. *On the Trial of Jesus.* Studia Judaica: Forschungen zur Wissenschaft des Judentums 1. Berlin: de Gruyter, 1961. Second edition: revised and edited by T. A. Burkill and G. Vermes, 1974.

> Assesses the Jewishness of Jesus and concludes that he was a Pharisee and was not condemned to death by the Sanhedrin, but by the Romans.

394 J. D. M. Derrett. *An Oriental Lawyer Looks at the Trial of Jesus and the Doctrine of Redemption.* London: School of Oriental and African Studies, University of London, 1966.

> While acknowledging that the Romans assumed the major part of responsibility, believes that some Jewish groups, for differing reasons, may have wished Jesus' death.

395 T. Horvath. "Why Was Jesus Brought to Pilate?" *NovT* 11 (1969) 174–84.

> Concludes that the Jewish leaders brought Jesus to Pilate in order that he might prove himself to be Israel's national deliverer.

396 E. Bammel (ed.). *The Trial of Jesus: Cambridge Studies in Honor of C. F. D. Moule.* SBT 2/13. Naperville, Ill.: Allenson/ London: SCM, 1970.

Fourteen essays concerned with various aspects of the trial of Jesus, including essays by D. R. Catchpole, "The Problem of the Historicity of the Sanhedrin Trial" (pp. 47–65); J. C. O'Neill, "The Charge of Blasphemy at Jesus' Trial before the Sanhedrin" (pp. 72–77); H. W. Hoehner, "Why Did Pilate Hand Jesus over to Antipas?" (pp. 84–90); W. Horbury, "The Trial of Jesus in Jewish Tradition" (pp. 103–21); R. Morgan, "'Nothing More Negative . . .': A Concluding Unscientific Postscript to Historical Research on the Trial of Jesus" (pp. 135–46); J. Blinzler, "The Jewish Punishment of Stoning in the New Testament Period" (pp. 147–61); and E. Bammel, "Crucifixion as a Punishment in Palestine" (pp. 162–65).

397 M. B. Chambers. "Was Jesus Really Obedient unto Death?" *JR* 50 (1970) 121–38.

Challenges R. Bultmann's view that Jesus suffered an emotional collapse when he realized that his death was unavoidable.

398 D. R. Catchpole. *The Trial of Jesus: A Study in the Gospels and Jewish Historiography from 1777 to the Present Day.* Studia Postbiblica 18. Leiden: Brill, 1971.

Concludes that Jesus had been arrested by Jewish guards and that the Sanhedrin met in order to find grounds for accusing him. Jesus was accused of claiming to be a son of God, was sentenced to death, and was delivered over to Pilate for execution of sentence.

399 *Judaism* 20 (1971) 10–74.

This issue of *Judaism* contains several contributions on the trial of Jesus by H. Cohn (pp. 10–23), M. S. Enslin (pp. 24–31), D. Flusser (pp. 32–36), R. M. Grant (pp. 37–42), S. G. F. Brandon (pp. 43–48), J. Blinzler (pp. 49–55), G. S. Sloyan (pp. 56–68), and S. Sandmel (pp. 69–74).

400 J. Wilkinson. "The Physical Cause of the Death of Christ." *ExpTim* 83 (1971–72) 104–7.

Concludes that Jesus' death came early because he voluntarily surrendered his life. See criticisms of this view offered by R. O. Ball and K. Leese in *ExpTim* 83 (1971–72) 248.

401 J. H. Charlesworth. "Jesus and Jehohanan: An Archaeological Note on Crucifixion." *ExpTim* 84 (1972–73) 147–50.

A description of the skeletal remains of one Jehohanan, who apparently was crucified between 6 C.E. and 66 C.E., and its relevance for understanding the crucifixion of Jesus; helpful bibliography.

402 G. S. Sloyan. *Jesus on Trial: The Development of the Passion Narratives and Their Historical and Ecumenical Implications.* Edited by J. Reumann. Philadelphia: Fortress, 1973.

Concludes that Jesus in all probability appeared before Jewish and Roman authorities, was mocked by Roman soldiers, and was denied by Peter. These are likely authentic traditions, for it is highly unlikely that the early church would have invented them.

403 J. G. Sobosan. "The Trial of Jesus." *Journal of Ecumenical Studies* 10 (1973) 70–93.

Argues that the gospel portrait of Pilate as weak and vacillating is not convincing; the crowd shouting for Jesus' crucifixion may have been supporters of Barabbas.

404 T. F. Glasson. "Davidic Links with the Betrayal of Jesus." *ExpTim* 85 (1973–74) 118–19.

Suggests that Davidic tradition may have colored the passion story, especially relating to Judas's act of betrayal.

405 P. E. Davies. "Did Jesus Die as a Martyr-Prophet?" *Biblical Research* 19 (1974) 37–47.

Concludes that Jesus was willing to accept death as a martyr-prophet.

406 F. Chenderlin. "Distributed Observance of the Passover—A Hypothesis." *Biblica* 56 (1975) 369–93.

The week of Jesus' death may have involved more than one set date for the observance of Passover. See also Chenderlin's article in *Biblica* 57 (1976) 1–24.

407 E. Rivkin. "Beth Din, Boulé, Sanhedrin: A Tragedy of Errors."
Hebrew Union College Annual 46 (1975) 181–99.
Argues that the Sanhedrin which interrogated Jesus was
not the *Beth Din* of his time, but the *Boulé*. For further
details see #412 below.

408 M. Hengel. *Crucifixion in the Ancient World and the Folly of
the Message of the Cross.* Translated by J. S. Bowden. Philadelphia: Fortress/London: SCM, 1977. Original title: "*Mors turp-
issima crucis*: Die Kreuzigung in der antiken Welt und die
'Torheit' des 'Wortes vom Kreuz.'" Pp. 125–84 in *Rechtferti-
gung: Festschrift für Ernst Käsemann zum 70. Geburtstag.* Edited by J. Friedrich, W. Pöhlmann, and P. Stuhlmacher. Tübingen: Mohr/Göttingen: Vandenhoeck & Ruprecht, 1976.
Significant discussion of Jesus' crucifixion and its background.

409 J. A. Fitzmyer. "Crucifixion in Ancient Palestine, Qumran
Literature, and the New Testament." *CBQ* 40 (1978) 493–
513. Reprinted in Fitzmyer's *To Advance the Gospel: New
Testament Studies,* pp. 125–46. New York: Crossroad, 1981.
Observes that recent archeological finds suggest that the
Romans may not have been the only people to have prac-
ticed crucifixion in the first century.

410 R. L. Overstreet. "Roman Law and the Trial of Christ." *Biblio-
theca Sacra* 135 (1978) 323–32.
Concludes that it was out of cowardice that Pilate gave in
to the demands for Jesus' death.

411 J. D. M. Derrett. "The Iscariot, *Mesira*, and the Redemption."
JSNT 8 (1980) 2–23.
Argues that Judas's betrayal was an act of *mesira*, the
handing over of a Jew to the Gentiles for punishment (as
Joseph had been handed over to Gentiles by his brothers).

412 E. Rivkin. *What Crucified Jesus? The Political Execution of
a Charismatic.* Nashville: Abingdon/London: SCM, 1984.
Argues that the Sanhedrin that condemned Jesus was not
the prestigious *Beth Din* (house of judgment), but an *ad
hoc* group of persons loyal to Caiaphas, himself an appoin-
tee of Pilate; believes that Pilate executed Jesus with little
concern over his guilt or innocence.

413 D. Hill. "Jesus before the Sanhedrin—On What Charge?" *Irish Biblical Studies* 7 (1985) 174–86.

Concludes that in all probability Jesus was crucified as a deceiver of the people.

414 F. Watson. "Why Was Jesus Crucified?" *Theology* 88 (1985) 105–12.

Argues that Jesus was likely crucified as a political criminal for speaking against the temple and having aroused great alarm among Jewish and Roman leaders.

415 O. Betz. "The Temple Scroll and the Trial of Jesus." *Southwest Journal of Theology* 30 (1988) 5–8.

11QTemple 6–13 shows that crucifixion was sometimes the penalty for threats against the temple.

416 V. K. Robbins. "The Crucifixion and the Speech of Jesus." *Forum* 4/1 (1988) 33–46.

Raises the question of the authenticity of Jesus' words before Pilate and from the cross (Matt 27:11–54; Mark 15:2–39; Luke 23:2–47; John 18:33–19:30; Gospel of Peter 1:1–5:20).

417 D. E. Garland. *One Hundred Years of Study on the Passion Narrative.* National Association of Baptist Professors of Religion Bibliographic Series 3. Macon, Ga.: Mercer University Press, 1989.

Provides 2,154 bibliographical entries (not annotated).

418 F. J. Matera. "The Trial of Jesus: Problems and Proposals." *Interp* 45 (1991) 5–16.

After discussing the synoptic data and the attendant problems, concludes that Pilate and the chief priests were responsible for Jesus' death.

10

Resurrection of Jesus

The interpretations of the resurrection of Jesus have run the gamut; virtually every theory conceivable has been proposed. R. Bultmann and pupils understood the resurrection as beyond the reach of historical criticism (*pace* E. Stauffer). The resurrected Jesus lives, it is argued, in the preaching of the kerygma. One of the major proponents for the bodily resurrection of Jesus is W. Pannenberg; note also the work of W. L. Craig, one of his students. Recently P. Lapide, a Jewish scholar, argued for the bodily resurrection of Jesus.

419 H. E. W. Turner. "The Resurrection." *ExpTim* 68 (1956–57) 369–71.

Rules out explanations that deny the reality of Jesus' resurrection; concludes that New Testament accounts are essentially reliable.

420 W. C. Robinson. "The Bodily Resurrection of Christ." *Theologische Zeitschrift* 13 (1957) 81–101.

Offers several lines of argument in defense of the bodily resurrection of Jesus.

421 C. F. D. Moule. "The Post-Resurrection Appearances in the Light of Festival Pilgrimages." *NTS* 4 (1957–58) 58–61.

Suggests that pilgrimages to festivals may account for the wide geographical range of postresurrection appearances.

422 J. Dupont. "Ressuscité le troisième jour." *Biblica* 40 (1959) 742–76.

Explores the origin of the "third day" tradition.

423 R. H. Fuller. "The Resurrection of Jesus Christ." *Biblical Research* 4 (1960) 8–24.

Concludes that the empty-tomb tradition is not historical, but arose in the early church as *didache* for new converts.

424 J. W. D. Smith. "The Resurrection of Christ: Myth or History?" *ExpTim* 72 (1960–61) 370–75.

Argues that the resurrection narratives contain elements of both myth and history.

425 E. C. Rust. "Interpreting the Resurrection." *Journal of Bible and Religion* 29 (1961) 25–34.

Argues that the evidence compels us to interpret the resurrection of Jesus as bodily.

426 R. A. Harrisville. "Resurrection and Historical Method." *Dialog* 1 (1962) 30–37.

Seeks a mediating position between the mythologizing approach of R. Bultmann on the one hand and the historicizing approach of E. Stauffer on the other.

427 G. E. Ladd. "Resurrection and History." *Dialog* 1 (1962) 55–56.

A reply to R. A. Harrisville (#426); see also #428.

428 G. E. Ladd. "The Resurrection and History." *Religion in Life* 32 (1963) 247–56.

Argues that Jesus' resurrection is a historical event, an instance of immortality breaking into the human sphere of mortality.

429 W. Marxsen et al. *The Significance of the Message of the Resurrection for Faith in Jesus Christ.* Edited by C. F. D. Moule. Translated by D. M. Barton and R. A. Wilson. SBT 2/8. Naperville, Ill.: Allenson/London: SCM, 1968. Original title: *Die Auferstehung Jesu als historisches und als theologisches Problem.* Gütersloh: Mohn, 1964. Reprinted in Marxsen et al.'s *Die Bedeutung der Auferstehungsbotschaft für den Glauben an Jesus Christ*, pp. 9–39. Gütersloh: Mohn, 1966.

In what proved to be a controversial essay, Marxsen argues that in "seeing" Jesus (1 Cor 15:8) the disciples did not actually see the risen Christ in a literal sense. The early community came to interpret the Easter experience in terms of resurrection ideas. In the German edition, responses are offered by U. Wilckens, "Die Überlieferungsgeschichte der Auferstehung Jesu" (pp. 41–63), and G. Delling, "Die Bedeutung der Auferstehung Jesu für den Glauben an Jesus Christus: Ein exegetischer Beitrag" (pp. 65–90), with a summary by H.-G. Geyer, "Die Auferstehung Jesu Christi: Ein Überblick über die Diskussion in der gegenwärtigen Theologie" (pp. 91–117).

430 H. Anderson. "The Easter Witness of the Evangelists." Pp. 35–55 in *New Testament in Historical and Contemporary Perspectives: Essays in Memory of G. C. H. Macgregor*. Edited by H. Anderson and W. Barclay. Oxford: Blackwell, 1965.

Argues that it is not profitable to attempt to reconstruct the sequence of Easter events. The importance of the resurrection narratives lies in their affirmation that the Jesus of history and the risen Christ are one and the same.

431 D. P. Fuller. *Easter Faith and History*. Grand Rapids: Eerdmans, 1965.

Appreciative of the work of W. Pannenberg (#432), argues for the historicity of the resurrection; sees this question as a major issue in the question of the historical Jesus.

432 W. Pannenberg. "Did Jesus Really Rise from the Dead?" *Dialog* 4 (1965) 128–35.

Argues that the resurrection of Jesus was a historical event, even though the word used to describe it—"resurrection"—is a metaphorical expression borrowed from apocalyptic.

433 P. Benoit. *The Passion and Resurrection of Jesus Christ*. Translated by B. Weatherhead. New York: Herder & Herder/ London: Darton, Longman & Todd, 1969. Original title: *Passion et Résurrection du Seigneur*. Lire la Bible 6. Paris: Cerf, 1966.

A detailed commentary on the passion and resurrection narratives of the Gospels; accepts the Fourth Gospel as reliable, even as based on eyewitness testimony.

434 D. P. Fuller. "The Resurrection of Jesus and the Historical Method." *Journal of Bible and Religion* 34 (1966) 18–24.

Concludes that Jesus was resurrected; historical method would suggest this conclusion because there is no Jewish understanding or expectation of an individual resurrection prior to the general resurrection.

435 J. H. Hayes. "Resurrection as Enthronement and the Earliest Church Christology." *Interp* 22 (1968) 333–45.

Argues that the earliest understanding of Jesus' resurrection was in terms of Davidic enthronement.

436 W. Marxsen. *The Resurrection of Jesus of Nazareth.* Translated by M. Kohl. Philadelphia: Fortress/London: SCM, 1970. Original title: *Die Auferstehung Jesu von Nazareth.* Gütersloh: Mohn, 1968.

Concludes that the confession "Jesus is risen" originally was not in reference to an event in the past; the resurrection tradition that emerges in the New Testament reflects an interpretation of Easter in terms of the human experience of living and dying. See also Marxsen's *Jesus and Easter: Did God Raise the Historical Jesus from the Dead?* (trans. V. P. Furnish; Nashville: Abingdon, 1990).

437 J. C. DeYoung. "Event and Interpretation of the Resurrection." Pp. 127–75 in *Interpreting God's Word Today.* Edited by S. Kistemaker. Grand Rapids: Baker, 1970.

From a conservative Reformed perspective criticizes various interpretations of the resurrection and its historicity in R. Bultmann, G. Bornkamm, W. Pannenberg, and others.

438 C. F. Evans. *Resurrection and the New Testament.* SBT 2/2. Naperville, Ill.: Allenson/London: SCM, 1970.

Concludes that the corporeality of Jesus' resurrection, though not important, cannot be ruled out.

439 R. H. Fuller. *The Formation of the Resurrection Narratives.*
New York/London: Macmillan, 1971. Second edition: Philadelphia: Fortress/London: SPCK, 1980.

Traces the development of earliest resurrection faith and
the development of the resurrection narratives, concluding that something outside of the disciples must have happened, something one might describe as "metahistorical."

440 A. Richardson. "The Resurrection of Jesus Christ." *Theology*
74 (1971) 146–54.

Interacting with W. Pannenberg and followers, believes
that the historical resurrection of Jesus is the only plausi-
ble explanation of the evidence.

441 W. O. Walker. "Christian Origins and Resurrection Faith."
JR 52 (1972) 41–55.

Explores the factors that contributed to early Christianity's understanding of Jesus' death and resurrection.

442 L. Sabourin. "The Resurrection of Jesus." *Biblical Theology
Bulletin* 5 (1975) 262–93.

Reviews several recent studies; concludes that scholars
are increasingly open to accepting the historicity of the
resurrection.

443 J. D. Crossan. "Empty Tomb and Absent Lord." Pp. 135–52
in *The Passion in Mark.* Edited by W. Kelber. Philadelphia:
Fortress, 1976.

Argues that the evangelist Mark "created the tradition of
the Empty Tomb as the precise and complete redactional
conclusion for his Gospel (16:1–8)" (p. 135).

444 J. P. Galvin. "Resurrection as *Theologia Crucis Jesu:* The
Foundational Christology of Rudolf Pesch." *Theological
Studies* 38 (1977) 513–25.

Reviews the dialogue between R. Pesch and others (see
Theologische Quartalschrift 153 [1973]) and notes that his
attempt to link Christology to the pre-Easter Jesus (and
not simply to Easter) is important and needs to be pursued.

445 P. Lapide. *The Resurrection of Jesus: A Jewish Perspective.*
Translated by W. C. Linss. Minneapolis: Augsburg/London:

SPCK, 1983. Original title: *Auferstehung: Ein jüdisches Glaubenserlebnis.* Stuttgart: Calwer/Munich: Kösel, 1977.

Argues that, although Jesus and his resurrection were a Jewish affair, the resurrection does not make him Israel's Messiah.

446 R. H. Stein. "Was the Tomb Really Empty?" *JETS* 20 (1977) 23–29.

Concludes that several compelling arguments can be made in favor of the gospel tradition that the tomb was found empty.

447 C. A. Evans. "Mark's Use of the Empty Tomb Tradition." *Studia Biblica et Theologica* 8/2 (1978) 50–55.

Pace J. D. Crossan (#443), concludes that the empty-tomb story in Mark's Gospel was not created by the evangelist, but derives from older tradition.

448 K. Grayston. "The Empty Tomb." *ExpTim* 92 (1980–81) 263–67.

Claims that the empty-tomb tradition is not essential to the resurrection tradition.

449 W. L. Craig. "The Empty Tomb of Jesus." Pp. 173–200 in *Studies of History and Tradition in the Gospels.* Edited by R. T. France. Gospel Perspectives 2. Sheffield: JSOT Press, 1981.

Argues that the evidence for the reliability of the empty-tomb tradition is compelling (see #450).

450 W. L. Craig. *The Son Rises: The Historical Evidence for the Resurrection of Jesus.* Chicago: Moody, 1981.

Elaborates on thesis in #449; surveys and rebuts alternative explanations (see #453).

451 G. R. Osborne. *The Resurrection Narratives: A Redactional Study.* Grand Rapids: Baker, 1984.

Accepts the essential historicity of the resurrection narratives; thinks that Mark's Gospel originally had an account of a resurrection appearance (which Osborne attempts to reconstruct on pp. 64–65).

452 P. Perkins. *Resurrection: New Testament Witness and Contemporary Reflection.* Garden City, N.Y./London: Doubleday, 1984.

A major study; compares the various Jewish beliefs about resurrection; concludes that the empty-tomb tradition (Mark 16:1–8) represents the evangelist's attempt to bring Jesus' earthly ministry to a close.

453 W. L. Craig. "The Historicity of the Empty Tomb of Jesus." *NTS* 31 (1985) 39–67.

Finds several lines of evidence that argue strongly for the historicity of the empty-tomb tradition (see #449).

454 S. T. Davis. "Was Jesus Raised Bodily?" *Christian Scholars Review* 14 (1985) 140–52.

Argues that there is no compelling evidence or reason to understand Jesus' resurrection in any other sense than bodily.

455 B. Lindars. "Jesus Risen: Bodily Resurrection But No Empty Tomb." *Theology* 89 (1986) 90–96.

Concludes that the empty-tomb tradition is inauthentic, part of later Christian interpretation of the resurrection of Jesus.

456 F. Watson. "'Historical Evidence' and the Resurrection of Jesus." *Theology* 90 (1987) 365–72.

Indisputable historical evidence for the resurrection cannot be adduced; for faith, all that is required is that the evidence not contradict the content of confession.

457 W. L. Craig. "Pannenbergs Beweis für Auferstehung Jesu." *Kerygma und Dogma* 34 (1988) 78–104.

Although accepting much of W. Pannenberg's position, it is argued that the historicity (or "extramental") aspect of Jesus' resurrection should not be denied.

458 J. P. Galvin. "The Origin of Faith in the Resurrection of Jesus: Two Recent Perspectives." *Theological Studies* 49 (1988) 25–44.

Interacting with R. Pesch and H. Verweyan, weaknesses and strengths are assessed.

459 G. O'Collins. *Interpreting the Resurrection: Examining the Major Problems in the Stories of Jesus' Resurrection.* New York: Paulist, 1988.

460 W. L. Craig. *Assessing the New Testament Evidence for the Historicity of the Resurrection of Jesus*. Studies in the Bible and the Early Church. Lewiston/Queenston: Mellen, 1989.

Concludes that the most reasonable explanation of the New Testament data is that Jesus did in fact rise from the dead.

461 C. E. B. Cranfield. "The Resurrection of Jesus Christ." *Exp-Tim* 101 (1989–90) 167–72.

Finding that the alternatives to the New Testament proclamation are not convincing, concludes that the best explanation is what the New Testament itself proclaims. For a critical response see G. T. Eddy in *ExpTim* 101 (1989–90) 327–29.

462 D. A. Walker. "Resurrection, Empty Tomb and Easter Faith." *ExpTim* 101 (1989–90) 172–75.

Concludes that the empty-tomb tradition cannot be easily dismissed.

11

Lives of Jesus

This chapter offers no more than a sampling of the thousands of lives of Jesus that have been written since the publication of Reimarus's fragments. Those included below either have made significant contributions to the scholarly quest of the historical Jesus or are representative of various schools of thought. The lives cited in chapter 2 are not repeated here; see especially H. S. Reimarus (#35), D. F. Strauss (#38), H. J. Holtzmann (#40), E. Rénan (#41), and C. H. Dodd (#60). For surveys see the following works in chapter 1: W. S. Kissinger (#26), D. L. Pals (#20), and A. Schweitzer (#7).

463 F. E. D. Schleiermacher. *The Life of Jesus.* Translated by S. M. Gilmour. Edited by J. C. Verheyden. Lives of Jesus Series. Philadelphia: Fortress, 1975. Original title: *Das Leben Jesu.* Edited by K. A. Rütenik. Berlin: Reimer, 1864.

   Most of the material comes from Schleiermacher's 1832 lecture notes; first major theologian to lecture publicly (beginning in 1819) on the scholarly problem of the life of Jesus; views Jesus as fully human.

464 F. Delitzsch. *A Day in Capernaum.* Translated by G. H. Schodde. New York: Funk & Wagnalls, 1887. Original title: *Ein Tag in Capernaum.* Leipzig: Naumann, 1873.

   Based on comparative background study; offers a portrait of what a typical day in Jesus' Galilean ministry would have been like.

465 F. W. Farrar. *Life of Christ*. New York: Dutton, 1874. Reprinted London: Hodder & Stoughton, 1989.

Translated into French, German, and many other languages. Perhaps the best of the Victorian lives of Jesus; believes that much of the gospel tradition derives from eyewitnesses.

466 B. Weiss. *The Life of Christ*. 3 vols. Translated by J. W. Hope. Edinburgh: T. & T. Clark, 1883–84. Original title: *Das Leben Jesu*. 2 vols. Berlin: Hertz, 1882. Reprinted Stuttgart/Berlin: Cotta, 1902.

Believes that Jesus' messianic consciousness gradually matured; only toward the end of his ministry did Jesus come to realize that he would have to die, for the death of the Baptist had opened up that possibility to his thinking.

467 A. Edersheim. *The Life and Times of Jesus the Messiah*. 2 vols. New York: Randolph/London: Longmans, 1883. Reprinted Grand Rapids: Eerdmans, 1943.

Rich with Jewish background; harmonizing approach.

468 O. Holtzmann. *The Life of Jesus*. Translated by J. T. Bealby and M. A. Canney. London: Black, 1904. Original title: *Das Leben Jesu*. Tübingen/Leipzig: Mohr, 1901.

Sees Jesus as a prophet and great teacher, but not as the supernatural Son of God; utilizes Mark, portions of Matthew, Luke, and the Gospel of the Hebrews.

469 W. Bousset. *Jesus*. Translated by J. P. Trevelyan. Crown Theological Library 14. New York: Putnam/London: Williams & Norgate, 1906. Reprinted 1911. Original title: *Jesus*. Halle: Gebauer-Schwetschke, 1904. Third edition: Tübingen: Mohr, 1907.

Argues that Jesus had a vision at his baptism, heard the voice of God speak, sensed his calling to preach, and went to Jerusalem with a "dim impulse and consciousness that there his destiny would be accomplished" (p. 15).

470 E. D. Burton. *The Life of Christ*. Chicago: University of Chicago Press, 1907.

Surveys background issues; describes a life of Jesus.

471 M. J. Lagrange. *The Gospel of Jesus Christ*. 2 vols. London: Burns, Oates, & Washbourne, 1938. Original title: *L'évangile de Jésus-Christ*. Paris: Gabalda, 1928.

Assessing the historical reliability of all four Gospels, produces a biography that attempts to assemble and harmonize all of the gospel materials.

472 C. A. H. Guignebert. *Jesus*. Translated by S. H. Hooke. London: Paul, Trench, Trübner, 1935. Reprinted New York: University Books, 1956. Original title: *Jésus*. Paris: Renaissance, 1933.

An engaging biographical account that is replete with critical questions and comments; amazingly insightful redaction-critical comments.

473 P. Gardner-Smith. *The Christ of the Gospels*. Cambridge: Heffer, 1938.

Believes that Jesus sensed his mission at his baptism and understood that his death would establish a new covenant.

474 E. J. Goodspeed. *A Life of Jesus*. New York: Harper, 1950. Reprinted Westport, Conn.: Greenwood, 1979.

Believes that Jesus journeyed to Jerusalem with hope of victory, yet anticipated rejection and death.

475 A. M. Hunter. *The Work and Words of Jesus*. Philadelphia: Westminster, 1950/London: SCM, 1951. Second edition: 1973.

Reviews the scholarly discussion, then sketches a life of Jesus, concluding that Jesus was aware of his mission as uniquely authorized of God and that his death would establish a new covenant.

476 T. W. Manson. *The Beginning of the Gospel*. New York/London: Oxford University Press, 1950.

A life of Jesus based on the Gospel of Mark, with interspersed paragraphs of comment.

477 V. Taylor. *The Life and Ministry of Jesus*. Nashville: Abingdon, 1955/London: Macmillan, 1954. Reprinted 1968.

Bases his life of Jesus on Mark's Gospel, a source believed to be essentially reliable; concludes that Jesus knew that

he was the Messiah, but not as the Jewish people understood it. Jesus journeyed to Jerusalem in anticipation of
rejection and death.

478 W. Barclay. *The Mind of Jesus*. New York: Harper & Row/
London: SCM, 1960.

One of the better popular books; to a great extent reflects
the thinking of the old quest; concludes that Jesus understood himself as the suffering Son of Man.

479 E. W. Bauman. *The Life and Teaching of Jesus*. Philadelphia:
Westminster, 1960.

Believes that the Gospels are essentially reliable; notes the
presence of "legend," behind which a kernel of history is
usually to be found; concludes that Jesus knew that he
faced death in Jerusalem.

480 E. W. Saunders. *Jesus in the Gospels*. Englewood Cliffs, N.J.:
Prentice-Hall, 1967.

A critical life of Jesus; argues that the "dominant consciousness of Jesus" was his belief that his destiny was to
suffer as the Lord's Servant.

481 E. F. Harrison. *A Short Life of Christ*. Grand Rapids: Eerdmans, 1968.

A life of Jesus based on all four Gospels, which are viewed
as reliable sources.

482 D. Guthrie. *Jesus the Messiah*. Grand Rapids: Zondervan/
London: Pickering & Inglis, 1972.

A life of Jesus written from a very conservative perspective; see also Guthrie's *Shorter Life of Christ* (Grand Rapids: Zondervan, 1978).

483 M. Burrows. *Jesus in the First Three Gospels*. Nashville: Abingdon, 1977.

Assumes that the Synoptic Gospels are essentially historical and that their chronology is historical.

484 J. Marsh. *Jesus in His Lifetime*. London: Sidgwick & Jackson,
1981.

Reviews the problem of the historical Jesus and Jesus'
background in Jewish Palestine; reconstructs what may be
known of Jesus' life; concludes that Jesus became aware of

his sonship at his baptism and sensed his mission to Israel
and to the Gentiles as well.

485 G. Theissen. *The Shadow of the Galilean: The Quest of the
Historical Jesus in Narrative Form.* Translated by J. S. Bowden. Philadelphia: Fortress/London: SCM, 1987. Original
title: *Der Schatten des Galiläers: Historische Jesusforschung
in erzählender Form.* Munich: Kaiser, 1986.

A narrative portrait of Jesus and his time; emphasizes
social and religious background.

12

Jesus in Noncanonical Historical Sources

The primary sources for the life of Jesus are, of course, the Gospels of the New Testament; however, there is some Jesus tradition elsewhere in the New Testament, most of which is found in Acts (1:4b–5, 7–8; 9:4b, 5b–6, 11–12, 15–16; 11:16b; 18:9b–10; 20:35b; 22:7b, 8b, 10b, 18b, 21; 23:11b; 26:14b, 15b–18), Paul's letters to the church at Corinth (1 Cor 7:10; 11:24b, 25b; 2 Cor 12:9a), and the Apocalypse (1:8a, 11; 1:17b–3:22; 22:7a, 12–13, 16, 20). In post–New Testament Christian writings the Jesus tradition is greatly expanded, mostly in the form of apocryphal gospels. In non-Christian circles, however, the Jesus tradition is limited, though what is extant is not without significance. Some scholars, most notably J. Jeremias, believe that some of the noncanonical tradition may very well derive from Jesus. Those sayings thought to be authentic are referred to as the *agrapha*, or "unwritten" sayings of Jesus (i.e., not written in the four canonical Gospels). Jeremias (#486, pp. 49–87) has identified twenty-one potentially authentic *agrapha*, of which a few examples are cited below:

> On the same day he saw a man performing a work on the Sabbath. Then he said to him: "Man! If you know what you are doing, you are blessed. But if you do not know, you are cursed and a transgressor of the law." (variant reading in Codex D inserted after Luke 6:5)

He who is near me is near the fire; he who is far from me is far from the kingdom. (from Origen, *Homilies on Jeremiah* 20:3; also found in the Gospel of Thomas 82)

No one can obtain the kingdom of heaven who has not passed through temptation. (from Tertullian, *On Baptism* 20)

You have rejected the living one who is before your eyes, and talk idly of the dead. (from Augustine, *Against the Enemy of the Law and the Prophets* 2:4:14)

There will be dissensions and squabbles. (from Justin, *Dialogue with Trypho* 35:3)

Ask for the great things, and God will add to you the little things. (first quoted by Clement of Alexandria, *Stromateis* 1:24:158)

Much of the remainder of the noncanonical tradition is, in contrast with the four Gospels, considerably more elaborate; some of it is fantastic, even grotesque. Following the general bibliography (§12.1), selections will be given from Christian apocryphal sources (§12.2), Gnostic sources (§12.3), Josephus (§12.4), Slavonic Josephus (§12.5), Hegesippus and the Josippon (§12.6), other Jewish sources (§12.7), Greco-Roman historians and writers (§12.8), Thallus (§12.9), Mara bar Serapion (§12.10), and the Qurʾan (§12.11).

12.1 General Bibliography

486 J. Jeremias. *Unknown Sayings of Jesus*. Translated by R. H. Fuller. London: SPCK, 1958. Second edition: 1964. Original title: *Unbekannte Jesusworte*. Gütersloh: Mohn, 1948. Fourth edition: 1965.

487 J. A. Fitzmyer. "The Oxyrhynchus *Logoi* of Jesus and the Coptic Gospel according to Thomas." *Theological Studies* 20 (1959) 505–60. Reprinted in Fitzmyer's *Essays on the Semitic Background of the New Testament*, pp. 355–433. London: Chapman, 1971.

488 F. F. Bruce. *Jesus and Christian Origins outside the New Testament*. Grand Rapids: Eerdmans/London: Hodder & Stoughton, 1974.

Surveys traditions pertaining to Jesus and Christian origins in pagan writers, Josephus, the rabbis, apocryphal gospels, the Qur'an and Islamic tradition, and archeology.

489 O. Hofius. "Unknown Sayings of Jesus." Pp. 336–60 in *The Gospel and the Gospels*. Edited by P. Stuhlmacher. Translated by J. S. Bowden. Grand Rapids: Eerdmans, 1991. Original title: "Unbekannte Jesusworte." Pp. 355–82 in *Das Evangelium und die Evangelien: Vorträge vom Tübinger Symposium 1982*. Edited by P. Stuhlmacher. WUNT 28. Tübingen: Mohr, 1983.

A critical assessment of the *agrapha*, in which it is concluded that it is doubtful "that the early Church freely, on a large scale, and without inhibitions, produced sayings of the earthly Jesus" (p. 359).

490 R. W. Funk. *New Gospel Parallels*. 2 vols. Philadelphia: Fortress, 1985.

A valuable tool providing a synopsis not only of the four New Testament Gospels, but of several other ancient "gospels" as well.

491 D. Wenham (ed.). *The Jesus Tradition outside the Gospels*. Gospel Perspectives 5. Sheffield: JSOT Press, 1985.

Several essays examine the Jesus tradition in Paul, James, 1 Peter, Gospel of Thomas, Apostolic Fathers, apocryphal gospels, early Jewish and classical authors; bibliography.

492 J. D. Crossan. *Sayings Parallels: A Workbook for the Jesus Tradition*. Foundations and Facet: New Testament. Philadelphia: Fortress, 1986.

Limited to "units which could or did exist in the tradition as isolated segments passed on in different contexts." Given this limitation, cites all instances of sayings in canonical and early extracanonical sources.

493 W. D. Stroker. *Extracanonical Sayings of Jesus*. Society of Biblical Literature Resources for Biblical Study 18. Atlanta: Scholars Press, 1989.

Extremely valuable tool that provides texts (Coptic, Greek, and Latin), translations, and helpful indexes; excellent bibliography.

494 C. A. Evans. "Jesus in Non-Christian Sources." Pp. 364–68 in *Dictionary of Jesus and the Gospels*. Edited by J. B. Green, S. McKnight, and I. H. Marshall. Downers Grove, Ill.: Inter-Varsity, 1992.

12.2 Christian Apocryphal Sources

The New Testament Apocrypha is made up of more than one hundred documents (see J. H. Charlesworth and J. R. Mueller, #501); many of these documents are "gospels," "acts," or "apocalypses." There are several fragmentary gospels (mostly deriving from Oxyrhynchus Papyri 1, 654, 655, 840, 1224, and Papyrus Egerton 2), various Jewish-Christian gospels (including the Gospel of the Nazarenes, the Gospel of the Ebionites, and the Gospel of the Hebrews), the infancy gospels, and dozens of other gospels named after various apostolic worthies (see M. R. James [#495], E. Hennecke [#496], and R. W. Funk [#490]). Two of the more significant noncanonical gospels are the Gospel of Peter (§12.2.1) and the Secret Gospel of Mark (§12.2.2).

495 M. R. James. *The Apocryphal New Testament*. Oxford: Clarendon, 1924. Corrected edition: 1953.

Provides translations of most New Testament Apocrypha.

496 E. Hennecke. *New Testament Apocrypha* (esp. vol. 1: "Gospels and Related Writings"). 2 vols. Edited by W. Schneemelcher. English translation edited by R. M. Wilson. Philadelphia: Westminster/London: Lutterworth, 1963, 1965. Original title: *Neutestamentliche Apokryphen*. 2 vols. Tübingen: Mohr, 1959–64. Fifth edition: 1988. Revised English edition of vol. 1: Louisville: Westminster/John Knox/Cambridge: Clarke, 1991.

Indispensable tool for the study of the New Testament Apocrypha; texts and bibliography. On the Gospel of Peter see vol. 1, pp. 183–87. In vol. 1, pp. 88–89, J. Jeremias cites eleven *agrapha* that he thinks have the strongest claim to authenticity.

497 M. Smith. *The Secret Gospel: The Discovery and Interpretation of the Secret Gospel according to Mark*. New York:

Harper & Row, 1973. Reprinted Wellingborough: Aquarian, 1985.

For a critical edition of the Secret Gospel of Mark, see Smith's *Clement of Alexandria and a Secret Gospel of Mark* (Cambridge: Harvard University Press, 1973). Smith's Secret Gospel may be a (modern?) forgery; cf. Q. Quesnell, "The Mar Saba Clementine: A Question of Evidence," *CBQ* 37 (1975) 48–67, and Quesnell's reply to Smith in *CBQ* 38 (1976) 200–203.

498 W. L. Lane. "A Critique of Purportedly Authentic Agrapha." *JETS* 18 (1975) 29–35.

Discusses criteria for determining the authenticity of the *agrapha*; concludes that when examined in light of these criteria, the best of the *agrapha* look doubtful. See #489 for a similar assessment.

499 R. Cameron. *The Other Gospels: Non-Canonical Gospel Texts.* Philadelphia: Westminster/Guildford: Lutterworth, 1982.

Texts of seventeen apocryphal gospels; annotated bibliography for each.

500 J. D. Crossan. *Four Other Gospels: Shadows on the Contours of Canon.* New York: Seabury, 1985.

A series of exegetical studies utilizing the Gospel of Thomas, Papyrus Egerton 2, the Secret Gospel of Mark, and the Gospel of Peter.

501 J. H. Charlesworth and J. R. Mueller. *The New Testament Apocrypha and Pseudepigrapha: A Guide to Publications, with Excurses on Apocalypses.* American Theological Library Association Bibliography Series 17. Metuchen, N.J.: Scarecrow/ American Theological Library Association, 1987.

A massive bibliography on the New Testament Apocrypha; lists over one hundred apocryphal texts.

12.2.1 Gospel of Peter

The Gospel of Peter (see #496, vol. 1, pp. 185–86) provides several large fragments narrating the death, burial, and resurrection of Jesus:

Now in the night in which the Lord's day dawned, when the soldiers, two by two in every watch, were keeping guard, there rang out a loud voice in heaven, and they saw the heavens opened and two men come down from there in a great brightness and draw near to the sepulcher. That stone which had been laid against the entrance to the sepulcher started of itself to roll and gave way to the side, and the sepulcher was opened, and both the young men entered in. When now those soldiers saw this, they awakened the centurion and the elders—for they also were there to assist the watch. And while they were relating what they had seen, they saw again three men come out from the sepulcher, and two of them sustaining the other, and a cross following them, and the heads of the two reaching to heaven, but that of him who was led of them by the hand overpassing the heavens. And they heard a voice out of the heavens crying, "You have preached to them that sleep." And from the cross there was heard the answer, "Yes." (9:35–10:42)

12.2.2 Secret Gospel of Mark

The Secret Gospel of Mark (from a letter of Clement of Alexandria to Theodore; see #497, pp. 16–17) allegedly provides additional information about the young man clothed with the linen cloth (cf. Mark 14:51–52), the very one who may have met the women at the tomb (cf. Mark 16:5). The relevant part of the fragment reads as follows:

And they came into Bethany, and a certain woman, whose brother had died, was there. And, coming, she prostrated herself before Jesus and says to him, "Son of David, have mercy on me." But the disciples rebuked her. And Jesus, being angered, went off with her into the garden where the tomb was, and straightway a great cry was heard from the tomb. And going near, Jesus rolled away the stone from the door of the tomb. And straightway, going in where the youth was, he stretched forth his hand and raised him, seizing his hand. But the youth, looking upon him, loved him and began to beseech him that he might be with him. And going out of the tomb they came into the house of the youth, for he was rich. And after six days Jesus told him what to do and in the evening the youth comes to him, wearing a linen cloth over [his] naked [body]. And he remained with him that night, for Jesus taught him the mystery of the kingdom of God. And thence, arising, he returned to the other side of the Jordan.

12.3 Gnostic Sources

The best known of the Coptic Gnostic sources is the Gospel of Thomas. The Coptic version appears to be a translation of a

Greek collection of sayings dating back to the second century, some fragments of which are extant (Oxyrhynchus Papyri 1, 654, and 655). In the Nag Hammadi library (hereafter cited as NHL) the Gospel of Thomas appears as the second tractate in codex 2 (pp. 32–51), divided by most scholars into 114 sayings. The tractate begins with the prologue: "These are the secret sayings which the living Jesus spoke and which Didymos Judas Thomas wrote down." Much of the material in Thomas parallels the New Testament Gospels (and other New Testament writings). Some of it is clearly later Gnostic tradition, while some of it may represent genuine dominical tradition (such as logion 82, cited above, and logia 64 and 65).

In most of the tractates in which Jesus appears he is presented as the mysterious revealer of heavenly knowledge and secrets; for example, in the Book of Thomas the Contender (NHL 2:7), the Sophia of Jesus Christ (NHL 3:4), the Apocalypse of Paul (NHL 5:2), the First Apocalypse of James (NHL 5:3), the Acts of Peter and the Twelve Apostles (NHL 6:1), the Apocalypse of Peter (NHL 7:3), the Letter of Peter to Philip (NHL 8:2), the Gospel of Mary (Berlin Gnostic Codex 8502:1), and in the two tractates cited below, the Apocryphon of James (§12.3.1) and the Apocryphon of John (§12.3.2).

502 A. Guillaumont et al. *The Gospel according to Thomas.* New York: Harper/Leiden: Brill, 1959.

Provides Coptic text and English translation of the Gospel of Thomas, with an index of biblical parallels.

503 E. M. Yamauchi. *Pre-Christian Gnosticism: A Survey of the Proposed Evidences.* Grand Rapids: Eerdmans/London: Tyndale, 1973. Second edition: Grand Rapids: Baker, 1983.

A scholarly assessment of the relationship of early Gnosticism and Christianity; criticizes the contention that New Testament Christology is substantially dependent upon Gnostic mythology or that Gnosticism antedates Christianity.

504 J. M. Robinson (ed.). *The Nag Hammadi Library.* San Francisco: Harper & Row/Leiden: Brill, 1977. Third edition: 1988.

An English translation of the entire (Coptic Gnostic) Nag Hammadi find, plus two related tractates (Berlin Gnostic Codex 8502:1, 4).

505 K. Rudolph. *Gnosis: The Nature and History of Gnosticism.* Translated by R. M. Wilson, P. W. Coxon, and K. H. Kuhn. San Francisco: Harper & Row/Edinburgh: T. & T. Clark, 1983. Original title: *Die Gnosis: Wesen und Geschichte einer spätantiker Religion.* Leipzig: Koehler & Amelang, 1977. Second edition: 1980.

A scholarly survey of the Gnostic literature (Coptic and Mandean); believes (*pace* E. M. Yamauchi in #503) that the New Testament understanding of Jesus has been significantly influenced by early Gnosticism.

12.3.1 Apocryphon of James

A typical example of the Gnostic tendency to view Jesus as the mysterious revealer of heavenly knowledge and secrets may be seen in the Apocryphon of James (see #504, pp. 30–31):

> The twelve disciples [were] all sitting together and recalling what the Savior had said to each one of them, whether in secret or openly, and [putting it] in books—[But I] was writing that which was in [my book]—lo, the Savior appeared, [after] departing from [us while we] gazed after him. And after 550 days since he had risen from the dead, we said to him, "Have you departed and removed yourself from us?"
>
> But Jesus said, "No, but I shall go to the place from whence I came. If you wish to come with me, come!"
>
> They all answered and said, "If you bid us, we come."
>
> He said, "Verily I say unto you, no one will enter the kingdom of heaven at my bidding, but (only) because you yourselves are full. Leave James and Peter to me that I may fill them." And having called these two, he drew them aside and bade the rest occupy themselves with that which they were about. (NHL 1:2:2:7–39)

12.3.2 Apocryphon of John

A similar account is found in the Apocryphon of John, a tractate that must have been quite popular in early Gnostic circles, judging by its appearance three times in the Nag Hammadi library (NHL 2:1, 3:1, 4:1). John, son of Zebedee and brother of James, was in the temple one day where he was asked by a Pharisee where his master had gone. "John" goes on to narrate (see #504, p. 105):

> [When] I, [John], heard these things [I turned] away from the tem-
> ple [to a desert place]. And I grieved [greatly in my heart saying],
> "How [then was] the Savior [appointed], and why was he sent [into
> the world] by [his Father] . . . ?"
> Straightway, [while I was contemplating these things], behold,
> the [heavens opened and] the whole creation [which is] below
> heaven shone, and [the world] was shaken. [I was afraid, and
> behold I] saw in the light [a youth who stood] by me. While I
> looked [at him he became] like an old man. And he [changed his]
> likeness (again), becoming like a servant. . . .
> He said to me, "John, John, why do you doubt, or why [are you]
> afraid? You are not unfamiliar with this image, are you?—that is,
> do not [be] timid!—I am the one who [is with you (pl.)] always. I
> [am the Father], I am the Mother, I am the Son. . . ." (NHL
> 2:1:1:17–2:14, supplemented from other texts)

12.4 Josephus

In two places according to Greek manuscripts of his works the first-century Jewish historian (Flavius) Josephus mentions Jesus (on John the Baptist, see *Jewish Antiquities* 18:5:2 §116–19). The passages are as follows (based on L. H. Feldman's translation in *Josephus* [Loeb Classical Library 433, 456; Cambridge: Harvard University Press/London: Heinemann, 1965], vol. 10, pp. 107–9; vol. 9, pp. 49–51, 495–99):

> And so he [Ananus the high priest] convened the judges of the San-
> hedrin and brought before them a man called James, the brother of
> Jesus who was called the Christ, and certain others. He accused
> them of having transgressed the law and delivered them up to be
> stoned. (*Jewish Antiquities* 20:9:1 §200–203)

> About this time there lived Jesus, a wise man, if indeed one ought
> to call him a man. For he was one who wrought surprising feats
> and was a teacher of such people as accept the truth gladly. He
> won over many Jews and many of the Greeks. He was the Messiah.
> When Pilate, upon hearing him accused by men of the highest
> standing among us, had condemned him to be crucified, those
> who had in the first place come to love him did not give up their
> affection for him. On the third day he appeared to them restored

to life, for the prophets of God had prophesied these and countless other marvelous things about him. And the tribe of Christians, so called after him, has still to this day not disappeared. (*Jewish Antiquities* 18:3:3 §63–64)

Although few dispute the authenticity of the first passage, most scholars suspect that the second passage, if not entirely an interpolation, has been edited by a later Christian. For if Josephus had truly believed the things found in this passage, then it is indeed strange that he mentions Jesus nowhere else. J. Klausner (#47, pp. 55–56) offered this hypothetical reconstruction (omitting Greek text and Klausner's parenthetical comments):

Now, there was about this time Jesus, a wise man; for he was a doer of wonderful works, a teacher of such men as receive the truth with pleasure. He drew over to him both many of the Jews and many of the Gentiles. And when Pilate, at the suggestion of the principal men among us, had condemned him to the cross, those that loved him at the first ceased not so [to do]; and the race of Christians, so named from him, are not extinct even now.

For a different emendation of this passage, see R. Eisler (#510). The question of the authenticity of this passage (known as the *Testimonium Flavium* [or *Flavianum*]), either in whole or in part, has been debated for centuries. Defenders of the authenticity of the passage include F. C. Burkitt (#506), A. Harnack (#507), and F. Dornseiff (#511). On the other hand, S. Zeitlin (#508) views the passage as an inauthentic interpolation. Those who view the passage as original, but redacted, include H. St. J. Thackeray (#509), S. G. F. Brandon (#512), Z. Baras (#515), and L. H. Feldman (#517). For other studies on the *Testimonium Flavium*, see P. Winter (#513), D. Hill (#516), and J. N. Birdsall (#518).

L. H. Feldman's observation (#517) that the *Testimonium Flavium* was apparently unknown to most of the early church fathers argues strongly for the inauthenticity of the present form of the passage, for had this form existed at the end of the first century it is quite likely that Christian apologists would have cited it often. Although Eusebius knows of this passage (*Ecclesiastical History* 1:11:7–8; *Demonstration of the Gospel* 3:5), according to Origen (*Commentary on Matthew* 10:50:17; *Against Celsus*

1:47) Josephus did not regard Jesus as the Messiah. The absence in the Arabic version, moreover, of the very lines suspected of being interpolations adds more support to the contention that the passage has been tampered with. The Arabic version of the *Testimonium Flavium* (cf. Agapius, *Book of the Title*) reads as follows (see #514, p. 16):

> Similarly Josephus the Hebrew. For he says in the treatises that he has written on the governance [?] of the Jews: "At this time there was a wise man who was called Jesus. And his conduct was good, and [he] was known to be virtuous. And many people from among the Jews and the other nations became his disciples. Pilate condemned him to be crucified and to die. And those who had become his disciples did not abandon his discipleship. They reported that he had appeared to them three days after his crucifixion and that he was alive; accordingly he was perhaps the Messiah concerning whom the prophets have recounted wonders."

506 F. C. Burkitt. "Josephus and Christ." *Theologisch Tijdschrift* 47 (1913) 135–44.

507 A. Harnack. "Der jüdische Geschichtschreiber Josephus und Jesus Christus." *Internationale Monatsschrift für Wissenschaft und Technik* 7 (1913) 1037–68.

See also Harnack's *Geschichte der altchristlichen Literatur bis Eusebius* (Leipzig: Hinrichs, 1893, 1897; reprinted 1958), vol. 1, pp. 858–60; vol. 2, p. 581.

508 S. Zeitlin. "The Christ Passage in Josephus." *Jewish Quarterly Review* 18 (1927–28) 231–55. Reprinted in Zeitlin's *Studies in the Early History of Judaism* (New York: Ktav, 1973), vol. 1, pp. 407–31.

For a general study see Zeitlin's *Josephus on Jesus* (#524) and his summary in *Jewish Quarterly Review* 21 (1930–31) 377–417.

509 H. St. J. Thackeray. *Josephus: The Man and the Historian*, pp. 136–49. New York: Jewish Institute of Religion, 1929. Reprinted New York: Ktav, 1967.

510 R. Eisler. *The Messiah Jesus and John the Baptist*, p. 62. Translated by A. H. Krappe. New York: Dial/London: Methuen, 1931. Original title: Ἰησοῦς βασιλεὺς οὐ βασιλεύσας:

*Die messianische Unabhängigkeitsbewegung vom auf-
treten Johannes des Täufers bis zum Untergang Jakobs des
Gerechten.* 2 vols. Religionswissenschaftliche Bibliothek 9.
Heidelberg: Winter, 1929–30.

511 F. Dornseiff. "Zum Testimonium Flavium." *Zeitschrift für
die neutestamentliche Wissenschaft* 46 (1955) 245–50.

512 S. G. F. Brandon. "The Testimonium Flavium." *History Today* 19 (1969) 438.

513 P. Winter. "Bibliography to Josephus, Antiquitates Judaicae,
xviii, 63, 64." *Journal of Historical Studies* 2 (1969–70) 292–
96.

514 S. Pines. *An Arabic Version of the Testimonium Flavianum
and Its Implications.* Jerusalem: Israel Academy of Sciences
and Humanities, 1971.

515 Z. Baras. "Testimonium Flavium: The State of Recent Scholarship." Pp. 303–13 and 378–85 in *Society and Religion in
the Second Temple Period.* Edited by M. Baras and Z. Baras.
Jerusalem: Masada, 1977.

516 D. Hill. "Jesus and Josephus' 'Messianic Prophets.'" Pp. 143–
54 in *Text and Interpretation: Studies in the New Testament
Presented to Matthew Black.* Edited by E. Best and R. M.
Wilson. Cambridge: Cambridge University Press, 1979.

517 L. H. Feldman. "The *Testimonium Flavium*: The State of the
Question." Pp. 179–99 and 288–93 in *Christological Perspec-
tives: Essays in Honor of Harvey K. McArthur.* Edited by
R. F. Berkey and S. A. Edwards. New York: Pilgrim, 1982.

518 J. N. Birdsall. "The Continuing Enigma of Josephus's Testimony about Jesus." *Bulletin of the John Rylands University
Library of Manchester* 67 (1984–85) 609–22.

12.5 Slavonic Josephus

In the Slavonic, or Old Russian, version of Josephus's *Jewish
War* several passages are found that make reference to the Baptist, Jesus, and early Christians (passages that are without paral-
lel in the Greek manuscripts of Josephus). Scholarly opinion is

divided over the question of their authenticity. A few of the most relevant passages include the following (see #519, pp. 106–10):

At that time also a man came forward—if even it is fitting to call him a man [simply]. His nature as well as his form were a man's; but his showing forth was more than [that] of a man. His works, that is to say, were godly, and he wrought wonder-deeds amazing and full of power. Therefore it is not possible for me to call him a man [simply]. But again, looking at the existence he shared with all, I would also not call him an angel.

And all that he wrought through some kind of invisible power, he wrought by word and command.

Some said of him, that our first Lawgiver has risen from the dead and shows forth many cures and arts. But others supposed [less definitely] that he is sent by God.

Now he opposed himself in much to the law and did not observe the Sabbath according to ancestral custom. Yet, on the other hand, he did nothing reprehensible nor any crime; but by word solely he effected everything.

And many from the folk followed him and received his teachings. And many souls became wavering, supposing that thereby the Jewish tribes would set themselves free from the Roman hands.

Now it was his custom often to stop on the Mount of Olives facing the city. And there also he avouched his cures to the people. And there gathered themselves to him 150 servants, but of the folk a multitude.

But when they saw his power, that he accomplished everything that he would by word, they urged him that he should enter the city and cut down the Roman soldiers and Pilate and rule over us. But that one scorned it.

And thereafter, when knowledge of it came to the Jewish leaders, they gathered together with the high priest and spake: "We are powerless and weak to withstand the Romans. But as withal the bow is bent, we will go and tell Pilate what we have heard, and we will be without distress, lest if he hear it from others, we be robbed of our substance and ourselves be put to the sword and our children ruined." And they went and told it to Pilate.

And he sent and had many of the people cut down. And he had that wonder-doer brought up. And when he had instituted a trial concerning him, he perceived that he is a doer of good, but not an evil-doer, nor a revolutionary, nor one who aimed at power, and set him free. He had, you should know, healed his dying wife.

And he went to his accustomed place and wrought his accustomed works. And as again more folk gathered themselves together round him, then did he win glory though his works more than all.

The teachers of the law were [therefore] envenomed with envy and gave thirty talents to Pilate, in order that he should put him to death. And he, after he had taken [the money], gave them consent that they should themselves carry out their purpose.

And they took him and crucified him according to the ancestral law. (inserted after *Jewish War* 2:9:3, between §174 and §175)

And over these tablets [at one of the gates leading into the temple] with inscriptions hung a fourth tablet with inscription in these [Greek, Roman, and Jewish] characters, to the effect: Jesus has not reigned as king; he has been crucified by the Jews because he proclaimed the destruction of the city and the laying waste of the temple. (an inscription concerning Jesus, inserted in *Jewish War* 5:5:2 §195)

[The temple curtain] had, you should know, been suddenly rent from the top to the ground, when they delivered over to death through bribery the doer of good, the man—yea, him who through his doing was no man. And many other signs they tell which came to pass at that time. And it was said that after he was put to death, yea after burial in the grave, he was not found. Some then assert that he is risen; but others, that he has been stolen by friends. I, however, do not know which speak more correctly. . . . But others said that it was not possible to steal him, because they had put guards all round his grave—thirty Romans, but a thousand Jews. (inserted after *Jewish War* 5:5:4 §214)

Some indeed by this understood Herod, but others the crucified wonder-doer Jesus, others say again Vespasian. (in reference to a prophecy of a coming world ruler, inserted at *Jewish War* 6:5:4, replacing §313)

519 G. R. S. Mead. *The Gnostic John the Baptizer*. London: Watkins, 1924.

See pp. 97–119 for discussion and English translation of the relevant passages peculiar to the Slavonic manuscripts.

520 H. St. J. Thackeray. "The Principal Additional Passages in the Slavonic Versions." Pp. 635–58 in *Josephus*, vol. 3. Loeb

Classical Library 210. Cambridge: Harvard University Press/ London: Heinemann, 1928.

Provides an English translation of relevant passages from Slavonic Josephus.

521 J. M. Creed. "The Slavonic Version of Josephus' History of the Jewish War." *Harvard Theological Review* 25 (1932) 277–319.

Studies the Slavonic "additions" and suspects that they are spurious.

522 R. Dunkerley. "The Riddles of Josephus." *Hibbert Journal* 53 (1954–55) 127–34.

Discusses the authenticity of the *Testimonium Flavium* and statements about Jesus in Slavonic Josephus; suspects that the Slavonic "additions" may derive from Josephus, but they are not necessarily historically well informed.

523 A. Rubinstein. "Observations on the Old Russian Version of Josephus' Wars." *Journal of Semitic Studies* 2 (1957) 329–48.

12.6 Hegesippus and the Josippon

The Josippon (or Yosippon) is a tenth-century (so D. Flusser, #526) or fourth-century (so S. Zeitlin, #524) narrative that describes the Second Temple period. The work is dependent upon a Latin translation of Josephus's *Jewish Antiquities* and a Latin adaptation of his *Jewish War* known as Hegesippus. Some manuscripts of the Josippon contain references to Jesus (e.g., "Yeshu the crucified one"; "rise up, brother, and eat, for the Son of Man has risen from the dead"), but they are likely late interpolations. There is one passage, found in MS Hebr. 1280 (fol. 123), that has a stronger claim to authenticity (from Eisler, #510, p. 97):

In those days there was much party strife and great disputes in Judea between the Pharisees and the "robbers" in Israel who followed Yeshuah ben Pandera the Nasorean, who did great miracles in Israel until the Pharisees overpowered him and hanged him on a pole.

524 S. Zeitlin. *Josephus on Jesus, with Particular Reference to Slavonic Josephus and the Hebrew Josippon*, pp. 52–60. Philadelphia: Dropsie College, 1931.

See also Zeitlin's article in *Jewish Quarterly Review* 53 (1962–63) 277–97.

525 A. A. Neuman. "A Note on John the Baptist and Jesus in Josippon." *Hebrew Union College Annual* 23 (1950–51) 137–49.

526 D. Flusser. "Josippon." Cols. 296–98 in *Encyclopedia Judaica*, vol. 10. Jerusalem: Keter/New York: Macmillan, 1971.

527 A. A. Bell Jr. "Classical and Christian Traditions in the Work of Pseudo-Hegesippus." *Indiana Social Studies Quarterly* 33 (1980) 60–64.

12.7 Other Jewish Sources

There are relatively few certain references to Jesus in the Talmud. Most of the references are of little historical value, for they usually represent nothing more than vague acquaintance with the Gospels or later polemic with Christians. A few of the references, however, may represent fairly early, independent, and possibly accurate tradition. The following passages, some of which are tannaic (i.e., from 50 B.C.E. to 200 C.E.), are accepted by most as referring to Jesus (see #530). In the following quotations, talmudic passages are adapted from I. Epstein's edition: *The Babylonian Talmud* (34 vols.; London: Soncino, 1935–48).

She [Mary] who was the descendant of princes and governors, played the harlot with carpenters [Joseph]. (Babylonian Talmud, tractate *Sanhedrin* 106a, apparently an allusion to the virginal birth of Jesus)

[The Angel of Death] said to his messenger, "Go, bring me Miriam [Mary] the women's hairdresser!" He went and brought him Miriam. (Babylonian Talmud, tractate *Hagiga* 4b; the word for "hairdresser" is *megaddela*, probably a reference to Mary Magdalene, who was sometimes confused with Mary the mother of Jesus)

When King Jannai [104–78 B.C.E.] slew our rabbis, R. Joshua and Jesus fled to Alexandria of Egypt. On the resumption of peace . . .

he arose, went, and found himself in a certain inn, where great honor was shown him. "How beautiful is this innkeeper!" Thereupon Jesus observed, "Rabbi, her eyes are narrow." "Wretch," he rebuked him, "do you engage yourself thus?" He sounded four hundred trumpets and excommunicated him. He [Jesus] came before him many times pleading, "Receive me!" But he would pay no heed to him. One day he [R. Joshua] was reciting the Shema', when Jesus came before him. He intended to receive him and made a sign to him. He [Jesus] thinking that it was to repel him, went, put up a brick, and worshiped it. "Repent," said he [R. Joshua] to him. He replied, "I have thus learned from you: 'He who sins and causes others to sin is not afforded the means of repentance.'" (Babylonian Talmud, tractate *Sanhedrin* 107b; cf. tractate *Sota* 47a)

Not like Elisha who thrust Gehazi away with both his hands, and not like Joshua ben Perahiah who thrust away Jesus the Nazarene with both his hands. (Babylonian Talmud, tractates *Sanhedrin* 107b and *Sota* 47a)

Jesus had five disciples: Matthai, Nakai, Nezer, Buni, and Todah. (Babylonian Talmud, tractate *Sanhedrin* 107b)

And a master has said, "Jesus the Nazarene practiced magic and led Israel astray." (Babylonian Talmud, tractate *Sanhedrin* 107b; cf. tractate *Sota* 47a; see also Tosepta, tractate *Shabbat* 11:15, and Babylonian Talmud, tractate *Shabbat* 104b)

One of the disciples of Jesus . . . told me, "Thus did Jesus the Nazarene teach me: 'For of the hire of a harlot has she gathered them, and to the hire of a harlot shall they return.'" (Babylonian Talmud, tractate *'Aboda Zara* 16b–17a; Tosepta, tractate *Hullin* 2:24; cf. *Qoheleth Rabbah* 1:8 §3; *Yalqut Shimeoni* on Micah 1 and Prov 5:8)

He [a judge] said to them, "I looked at the end of the book, in which it is written, 'I am not come to take away the Law of Moses and I am not come to add to the law of Moses' [cf. Matt 5:17], and it is written, 'Where there is a son, a daughter does not inherit.'" She said to him, "Let your light shine forth as a lamp" [cf. Matt 5:16]. R. Gamaliel said to her, "The ass came and kicked the lamp over." (Babylonian Talmud, tractate *Shabbat* 116b)

On the eve of Passover they hanged Jesus the Nazarene. And a herald went out, in front of him, for forty days saying: "He is going to be stoned, because he practiced sorcery and enticed and led Israel astray. Anyone who knows anything in his favor, let him come and plead in his behalf." But, not having found anything in his favor, they hanged him on the eve of Passover. (Babylonian Talmud, tractate *Sanhedrin* 43a)

Woe to him who makes himself alive by the name of God. (Babylonian Talmud, tractate *Sanhedrin* 106a, possibly an allusion to Jesus' resurrection)

He then went and raised Jesus by incantation. (Babylonian Talmud, tractate *Giṭṭin* 57a, MS M)

It once happened that ben Dama, the son of R. Ishmael's sister, was bitten by a serpent; and Jacob [James?], a native of Kefar Sekaniah, came to him in the name of Jesus ben Pantera. But R. Ishmael did not permit him. (Tosepta, tractate *Ḥullin* 2:22)

528 G. H. Dalman and H. Laible. *Jesus Christ in the Talmud, Midrash, Zohar, and the Liturgy of the Synagogue.* Translated and edited by A. W. Streane. Cambridge: Deighton, Bell, 1893. Reprinted New York: Arno, 1973. Original titles: G. H. Dalman. *Was sagt der Thalmud über Jesum?* Schriften des Institutum Judaicum in Berlin 11. Berlin: Reuther, 1891; AND H. Laible. *Jesus Christus im Thalmud.* Schriften des Institutum Judaicum in Berlin 10. Leipzig: 1891. Second edition: 1900.

In the English translation Laible's work is supplemented by new work by Dalman. Although dated, this is an excellent survey; talmudic passages are cited in both the original language and English translation

529 G. H. Dalman. *The Words of Jesus: Considered in the Light of Post-Biblical Jewish Writings and the Aramaic language.* Translated by D. M. Kay. Edinburgh: T. & T. Clark, 1902. Original title: *Die Worte Jesu, mit Berücksichtigung des nachkanonischen jüdischen Schriftums und der aramäischen Sprache,* vol. 1. Leipzig: Hinrichs, 1898. Second edition: 1930.

530 R. T. Herford. *Christianity in Talmud and Midrash*. London: Williams & Norgate, 1903. Reprinted New York: Ktav, 1975.

A classic study; most of the examples cited above come from this work.

531 M. Goldstein. *Jesus in the Jewish Tradition*. New York: Macmillan, 1950.

532 W. Ziffer. "Two Epithets for Jesus of Nazareth in Talmud and Midrash." *Journal of Biblical Literature* 85 (1966) 356–59.

Suggests that the names Ben Stada and Ben Pandira, epithets sometimes applied to Jesus in the Talmud and midrashim, are really to be understood as Ben Satana and Ben Pandora.

533 J. Maier. *Jesus von Nazareth in der talmudischen Überlieferung*. Erträge der Forschung 82. Darmstadt: Wissenschaftliche Buchgesellschaft, 1978.

12.8 Greco-Roman Historians and Writers

There are only a few references to Jesus and early Christianity in early Greco-Roman historians and writers. They are as follows (see #535, pp. 163–78):

This name [i.e., "Christian"] originates from "Christus" who was sentenced to death by the procurator Pontius Pilate during the reign of Tiberius. This detestable superstition, which had been suppressed for a while, spread anew not only in Judea where the evil had started, but also in Rome, where everything that is horrid and wicked in the world gathers and finds numerous followers. (Tacitus, *Annals* 15:44; 110–120 c.e.)

Claudius expelled the Jews from Rome who, instigated by Chrestus [*sic*], never ceased to cause unrest. (Suetonius, *Claudius* 25:4; 110–120 c.e.; there are two basic interpretations of this passage: the "Jews" may really refer to Christians, who in the first century were viewed as no more than a sect within Judaism itself, or the designation may refer to Jews who quarreled with Christians [along the lines of what we see in Acts]; "Chrestus" is probably an error arising from confusing the word *chrestus* with the title *Christus*, a title with which a Roman would not be familiar)

They [the Christians] assured me that the sum total of their guilt or their error consisted in the fact that they regularly assembled on a certain day before daybreak. They recited a hymn antiphonally to Christ as (their) God and bound themselves with an oath not to commit any crime, but to abstain from theft, robbery, adultery, breach of faith, and embezzlement of property entrusted to them. After this it was their custom to separate, and then to come together again to partake of a meal, but an ordinary and innocent one. (Pliny the Younger, *Epistles* 10:96 [to Emperor Trajan]; 110 C.E.)

[Christians] still worship the man who was crucified in Palestine because he introduced a new cult into the world. . . . [Christians are] worshiping that crucified sophist himself and living under his laws. (Lucian of Samosata, *Peregrinus* §§11, 13; ca. 115–ca.200)

It was by magic that he [Jesus] was able to do the miracles which he appeared to have done. (Celsus, as quoted by Origen, *Against Celsus* 1:6; see #534, p. 10)

He [Jesus] was brought up in secret and hired himself out as a workman in Egypt, and after having tried his hand at certain magical powers he returned from there, and on account of those powers gave himself the title of God. (Celsus, as quoted by Origen, *Against Celsus* 1:38; see #534, p. 37)

These were the actions of one hated by God and of a wicked sorcerer. (Celsus, as quoted by Origen, *Against Celsus* 1:71; see also 1:68; see #534, p. 65)

534 H. Chadwick. *Origen: Contra Celsum*. Cambridge: Cambridge University Press, 1953. Reprinted 1965.

535 H. Conzelmann. *History of Primitive Christianity*. Translated by J. E. Steely. Nashville: Abingdon/London: Darton, Longman & Todd, 1973. Original title: *Geschichte des Urchristentums*. Göttingen: Vandenhoeck & Ruprecht, 1969.

12.9 Thallus

Thallus (*History* 3; 50 C.E.), known as the Samaritan Chronicler, makes reference to the darkness at the time of Jesus' crucifixion (see Mark 15:33). Julius Africanus (died after 240 C.E.)

reports (taken from fragment 18 of Africanus's five-volume *Chronography*, preserved in Georgius Syncellus's *Chronology*; see #536, vol. 6, p. 136):

> This darkness Thallus, in the third book of his *History*, calls, as appears to me without reason, an eclipse of the sun.

536 A. Roberts and J. Donaldson (eds.). *The Ante-Nicene Fathers.* 10 vols. Edinburgh: T. & T. Clark, 1885. Reprinted Grand Rapids: Eerdmans, 1951; 1986.

12.10 Mara bar Serapion

Mara bar Serapion writes in a letter to his son (ca. 73 C.E.; see #537, p. 73):

> For what advantage did . . . the Jews [gain] by the death of their wise king, because from that same time their kingdom was taken away?

537 W. Cureton. *Spicilegium Syriacum.* London: Rivingtons, 1855.

> See also R. Dunkerley, *Beyond the Gospels* (Baltimore: Penguin, 1957), p. 27.

12.11 Qurʾan

"Jesus son of Mary" (*Isa ibn Maryam*) is mentioned several times in the Qurʾan (ca. 620). For a convenient assessment see F. F. Bruce (#488, pp. 167–77). The Arabic tradition appears to be dependent upon the New Testament Gospels, especially Luke (compare Qurʾan 3:37–41 with Luke 1:5–25, 57–79). Consider the following allusions (adapted from #538):

> When a woman of Imran said: "My Lord! Surely I vow to you what is in my womb, to be devoted (to your service). Accept therefore from me. Surely you are the Hearing, the Knowing." So when she brought forth, she said: "My Lord! Surely I have brought forth a female"—and Allah knew best what she brought forth—"and the male is not like the female, and I have named it Mary, and I com-

mend her and her offspring into your protection from the accursed
Satan." (3:35–36, on the birth and naming of Mary)

And when the angels said: "O Mary! Surely Allah has chosen you
and purified you and chosen you above the women of the world.
. . ." When the angels said: "O Mary, surely Allah gives you good
news with a word from him whose name is the Messiah, Jesus son
of Mary, worthy of regard in this world and the hereafter and of
those who are made near (to Allah). And he shall speak to the people when in the cradle and when of old age, and (he shall be) one
of the good ones." She said: "My Lord! When shall there be a son
(born) to me, and man has not touched me?" He said: "Even so,
Allah creates what he pleases; when he has decreed a matter, he
only said to it, 'Be,' and it is. And he will teach him the Book and
the wisdom and the Tavrat and the Injeel, and (make him) an apostle to the children of Israel, saying, 'I have come to you with a sign
from your Lord, that I determine for you out of dust like the form
of a bird, then I breathe into it and it becomes a bird with Allah's
permission and I heal the blind and the leprous, and bring the dead
to life with Allah's permission and I inform you of what you
should eat and what you should store in your houses.'" (3:42, 45–
49, on the virginal conception and birth of Jesus; see also 3:59;
compare Luke 1:28–38, 42)

And mention Mary in the Book when she drew aside from her fam-
ily to an eastern place, taking a veil (to screen herself) from them.
Then we [Allah] sent to her our spirit, and there appeared to her a
well-made man. . . . She said: "When shall I have a boy and no
mortal has yet touched me, nor have I been unchaste?" . . . So she
conceived him; then withdrew herself with him to a remote place.
And the throes (of childbirth) compelled her to betake herself to
the trunk of a palm tree. She said: "Oh, would that I had died
before this, and had been a thing quite forgotten!" Then (the child)
called out to her from beneath her: "Grieve not." (19:16–17, 20,
22–24; see also 66:12)

When the disciples said: "O Jesus son of Mary, will your Lord consent to send down to us food from heaven?" He said: "Be careful
of (your duty to) Allah, if you are believers." They said: "We desire
that we should eat of it and that our hearts should be at rest, and
that we may know that you have indeed spoken the truth to us
that we may be of the witnesses to it." Jesus the son of Mary said:
"O Allah, our Lord! Send down to us food from heaven which

should be to us an ever-recurring happiness, to the first of us and to the last of us, and a sign from you, and grant us means of subsistence, and you are the best of the providers." Allah said: "Surely I will send it down to you, but whoever shall disbelieve afterward from among you, surely I will chastise him with a chastisement with which I shall not chastise anyone among the nations." (5:117–18, on the feeding of the five thousand; compare John 6:31–65)

And when Allah will say: "O Jesus son of Mary! Did you say to men, 'Take me and my mother for two gods besides Allah'? He will say: 'Glory be to you, it did not befit me that I should say what I had no right to (say). If I had said it, you would indeed have known it. You know what is in my mind, and I do not know what is in your mind. Surely you art the great knower of the unseen things.'" (5:119, on Jesus' denial of his divine sonship and Mary's deity; see also 5:71, 75; 4:171)

Allah set a seal upon them owing to their unbelief, so they shall not believe except a few—for their saying: "Surely we have killed the Messiah, Jesus son of Mary, the apostle of Allah." They did not kill him, nor did they crucify him, but it appeared to them (like Jesus) . . . Nay! Allah took him up to himself. (4:155–158, on the death and ascension of Jesus; a similar idea is credited to Basilides, according to Irenaeus, *Against Heresies* 1:24:4 [adapted from #536, vol. 1, p. 349]: "He [Christ] appeared, then, on earth as a man, to the nations of these powers, and wrought miracles. Wherefore he did not himself suffer death, but Simon, a certain man of Cyrene, being compelled, bore the cross in his stead; so that this latter being transfigured by him, that he might be thought to be Jesus, was crucified, through ignorance and error, while Jesus himself received the form of Simon, and, standing by, laughed at them.")

538 M. H. Shakir. *Holy Qur'an*. Elmhurst, N.Y.: Tahrike Tarsile Qur'an, 1983.
       Contains English translation and Arabic text.

13

Jesus and John the Baptist

In recent years scholars have come to recognize the importance of John the Baptist (or Baptizer) for life-of-Jesus research. The discovery of Qumran, moreover, has revealed the similarity of language and world view with reference to Jesus, John, and the Dead Sea sectarians. Indeed, the discovery of Qumran has rendered obsolete Baptist research prior to 1950. Since at some point in his life Jesus had some sort of relationship with John, it follows that the more one can learn about John, the more one learns, at least by inference, about Jesus and his earliest followers.

539 J. Jeremias. "Ἠλ(ε)ίας." Pp. 928–41 in *Theological Dictionary of the New Testament*, vol. 2. Edited by G. Kittel. Translated and edited by G. W. Bromiley. Grand Rapids: Eerdmans, 1964. Original title: "Ἠλ(ε)ίας." Pp. 930–43 in *Theologisches Wörterbuch zum Neuen Testament*, vol. 2. Edited by G. Kittel. Stuttgart: Kohlhammer, 1935.

Surveys primary literature and probes in what ways Elijah tradition influenced the ministries of John and Jesus and how they were later interpreted by their followers.

540 W. H. Brownlee. "John the Baptist in the New Light of Ancient Scrolls." *Interp* 9 (1955) 71–90. Reprinted in *The Scrolls and the New Testament*, pp. 33–53, 252–56. Edited by K. Stendahl. New York: Harper & Row, 1957/London: SCM, 1958. Reprinted Westport, Conn.: Greenwood, 1975.

One of the first studies in which the New Testament and Josephan portraits of John are compared to the Qumran scrolls; concludes that John had been an Essene.

541 A. S. Geyser. "The Youth of John the Baptist." *NovT* 1 (1956) 70–75.

Thinks it likely that John spent some of his youth among the Essenes.

542 J. A. T. Robinson. "The Baptism of John and the Qumran Community." *Harvard Theological Review* 50 (1957) 175–91. Reprinted in Robinson's *Twelve New Testament Studies*, pp. 11–27. SBT 34. Naperville, Ill.: Allenson/London: SCM, 1962.

Concludes that it is probable that the Baptist had been a member of the Qumran community, and that Jesus' ministry embodied Qumran's self-understanding of a purified and prepared Servant of the Lord who would atone for Israel.

543 J. A. T. Robinson. "Elijah, John and Jesus: An Essay in Detection." *NTS* 4 (1957–58) 263–81. Reprinted in Robinson's *Twelve New Testament Studies*, pp. 28–52. SBT 34. Naperville, Ill.: Allenson/London: SCM, 1962.

Argues that John preached Jesus as the Elijah who was to come, but later became disillusioned. Jesus, viewing John as Elijah, portrayed himself as the Lord's Servant.

544 J. Pryke. "John the Baptist and the Qumran Community." *Revue de Qumran* 4 (1964) 483–96.

Explaining away the major similarities, doubts that John had anything to do with the Qumran community.

545 C. H. H. Scobie. *John the Baptist*. London: SCM, 1964.

Accepts most of the New Testament data as reliable (including the Lucan infancy narrative); examines every facet of John's life, ministry, martyrdom, and the subsequent history of the Baptist movement.

546 A. G. Patzia. "Did John the Baptist Preach a Baptism of Fire and the Holy Spirit?" *Evangelical Quarterly* 40 (1968) 21–27.

As is seen from Old Testament prophetic precedence, concludes that John's preaching included the promise of the outpouring of the Holy Spirit, and not only the impending threat of judgment.

547 W. Wink. *John the Baptist in the Gospel Tradition.* SNTSMS 7. Cambridge: Cambridge University Press, 1968.

Explores how Q and the four evangelists made use of the Baptist tradition and concludes that Jesus assessed John very positively, arguing that through John's influence "Jesus perceived the nearness of the kingdom and his own relation to its coming" (p. 113).

548 O. Böcher. "Ass Johannes der Täufer kein Brot (Luk. vii.33)?" *NTS* 18 (1971–72) 90–92.

Argues that John's diet was that of a prophet who wished to avoid the potentially negative effects of meat and wine.

549 J. D. G. Dunn. "Spirit-and-Fire Baptism." *NovT* 14 (1972) 81–92.

Concludes that John's preaching involved grace ("Spirit") and judgment ("fire").

550 J. H. Hughes. "John the Baptist: The Forerunner of God Himself." *NovT* 14 (1972) 191–218.

Argues that John was the preparer for Yahweh's coming in judgment (with the sandals saying derived from Ps 60:8 and 108:9, but later misunderstood by Christians), but after his death came to be interpreted by Jesus as Elijah revived. Later Christians saw John as Jesus' forerunner.

551 J. Reumann. "The Quest for the Historical Baptist." Pp. 181–99 in *Understanding the Sacred Text: Essays in Honor of Morton S. Enslin on the Hebrew Bible and Christian Beginnings.* Edited by J. Reumann. Valley Forge, Penn.: Judson, 1972.

Interacting with W. Wink (#547), J. A. T. Robinson (#542, #543), and others, argues for more critical methods in assessing what can be known about John and Jesus.

552 E. W. Burrows. "Did John the Baptist Call Jesus 'the Lamb of God'?" *ExpTim* 85 (1973–74) 245–49.

Argues that there are good grounds for the authenticity of John's saying.

553 M. S. Enslin. "John and Jesus." *Zeitschrift für die neutesta-mentliche Wissenschaft* 66 (1975) 1–18.

Argues that Jesus was never a disciple of John, though the former may have launched his public ministry in the wake of the latter's execution. Asserts that the gospel portraits of John are unreliable.

554 J. L. Martyn. "We Have Found Elijah." Pp. 181–219 in *Jews, Greeks and Christians: Religious Cultures in Late Antiquity: Essays in Honor of William David Davies.* Edited by R. Hamerton-Kelly and R. Scroggs. Studies in Judaism in Late Antiquity 21. Leiden: Brill, 1976.

Argues that a pre-Johannine Christology identified Jesus with Elijah, though this strand was suppressed by the fourth evangelist.

555 J. A. Fitzmyer. *The Gospel according to Luke I–IX,* pp. 388–89, 453–54, 459–60. Anchor Bible 28. Garden City, N.Y.: Doubleday, 1981.

A succinct survey of the principal evidence of John's relationship to the Essenes and of his relationship to Jesus, concluding that John likely had spent some of his youth among Essenes.

556 P. W. Hollenbach. "The Conversion of Jesus: From Jesus the Baptizer to Jesus the Healer." Pp. 196–219 in *Aufstieg und Niedergang der römischen Welt,* section 2: *Principat,* vol. 25: *Religion (Vorkonstantinisches Christentum: Leben und Umwelt Jesu; Neues Testament [Kanonische Schriften und Apokryphen]),* part 1. Edited by W. Hasse. Berlin: de Gruyter, 1982.

Argues that Jesus ceased baptizing in the tradition of John the Baptist when he experienced a new vision, a new sense of mission.

557 S. L. Davies. "John the Baptist and Essene Kashruth." *NTS* 29 (1983) 569–71.

Suspects that John's unusual diet had to do with his desire to observe the Essenes' strict *kashruth.*

558 E. Rivkin. "Locating John the Baptizer in Palestinian Judaism: The Political Dimension." *SBLSP* 22 (1983) 79–85.

Believes that John and Jesus, because of their large followings, were viewed by the Romans as dangerous subversives and that the Romans could not risk trying to make a distinction between leaders who drew crowds for purposes of sedition (such as Judas and Theudas) and those who drew crowds for spiritual renewal (such as John and Jesus).

559 C. R. Kazmierski. "The Stones of Abraham: John the Baptist and the End of Torah (Matt 3,7–10 par. Luke 3,7–9)." *Biblica* 68 (1987) 22–40.

Argues that the Baptist did not utter these words, but that they are the words of a later Christian prophet.

560 B. Reicke. "The Historical Setting of John's Baptism." Pp. 209–24 in *Jesus, the Gospels, and the Church: Essays in Honor of William R. Farmer.* Edited by E. P. Sanders. Macon, Ga.: Mercer University Press, 1987.

The respective messages of John and Jesus were not the same, though both spoke of God's kingdom. Whereas the former clearly anticipated a coming one, the latter did not.

561 B. Witherington III. "Jesus and the Baptist—Two of a Kind?" *SBLSP* 27 (1988) 225–44.

Early in his ministry Jesus probably worked with John, but, unlike John, he did not anticipate a successor. Rather, Jesus saw himself as "bringing about the final eschatological message and work of God for his people Israel" (p. 243).

562 S. J. Nortjé. "John the Baptist and Resurrection Traditions in the Gospels." *Neotestamentica* 23 (1989) 349–58.

Concludes that Jesus was identified as a revived John, who in turn had earlier been identified as a revived Elijah.

563 W. B. Badke. "Was Jesus a Disciple of John?" *Evangelical Quarterly* 62 (1990) 195–204.

Concludes that although Jesus was a disciple of John, the Baptist probably recognized Jesus as the coming one, the fulfillment of his prophetic proclamation, and so gathered disciples to send to Jesus.

564 O. Betz. "Was John the Baptist an Essene?" *Bible Review* 6/6 (1990) 18–25.

Concludes that John had been raised in an Essene community.

565 J. Murphy-O'Connor. "John the Baptist and Jesus: History and Hypotheses." *NTS* 36 (1990) 359–74.

Argues that initially Jesus' ministry was an extension of John's, but at some point it changed radically.

566 R. L. Webb. *John the Baptizer and Prophet: A Socio-Historical Study.* Journal for the Study of the New Testament Supplement 62. Sheffield: JSOT Press, 1991.

Major study; concludes that John's ministry implied the anticipation of repossessing and cleansing the land of Israel and that John may have been the forerunner of Jesus.

Index to Modern Authors

Authors' works are noted with plain numbers (i.e., roman type). Italicized numbers indicate that the scholar is mentioned in either the bibliographic entry or the annotation. Numbers in parentheses indicate pages.

Index to Ancient Writings

Italicized numbers indicate entries. Numbers in parentheses indicate pages.

Other Ancient Writings and Writers